GOLD REFINING.

DONALD CLARK, M.M.E.

❧ ❧ ❧

CRITCHLEY PARKER.
AUSTRALIAN MINING STANDARD,
AUSTRALIA AND LONDON.

SIR ISAAC PITMAN & SONS, LIMITED,
1 AMEN CORNER, E.C.
LONDON.

1909.

Printed in Australia.

CONTENTS.

CHAPTER I.

Occurrence of Native Gold.
    Simple Methods of Purification.
    Amalgam in Battery Boxes.
    Amalgam in Pans.
    Amalgum from Copper Plates.
    The Purification of Mercury.
    Refining Retorted God.

CHAPTER II.

Refining Gold with Oxidising and Chloridising Agents.
    Nitre Refining.
    Refining with Mercuric Chloride.
    Refining with Ammonium Chloride.
    Refining with Iron.
    Refining with Sodium Bisulphate.
    Refining with Sodium Bisulphate and Salt.
    Refining with Boric and Phosphoric Acids.
    Refining with Boric Acid and Oxidising Agents.
    Refining with Phosphoric Acid and Oxidising Agents.

CHAPTER III.

Sulphur Refining.
    Refining with Sulphur Alone.
    Refining with Sulphur and Other Metals.
    Refining with Sulphur and Sodium.
    Refining with Sulphide of Antimony.
    Removal of Copper from Cyanide Bullion with Sulphur.

CHAPTER IV.

Refining with Cementation Processes.
    Older Processes with Nitre.
    Older Processes with Common Salt.

CHAPTER V.

Refining Gold Bullion by Means of Oxygen or Air.
Dr. T. Kirk Rose's Experiments with Oxygen and Air.
Work Done in Western Australia.

CHAPTER VI.

Miller's Process of Refining.
    History of the Process.
The Methods Adopted at the Melbourne Mint.
    Receiving Gold.
    Construction of Melting Furnaces.
    The Crucibles and Their Connections.
    The Chlorine Generators.
    Details of the Whole Operation.
    Recovery of the Silver.

CHAPTER VII.

Parting with Nitric Acid—Experimental Work.
    Parting with Silver as the Alloying Metal.
    Parting with Zinc as the Alloying Metal.
    Parting with Sodium as the Alloying Metal.

GOLD REFINING.

CHAPTER VIII.
Parting with Nitric Acid on a Large Scale.
Silver-Gold Alloys.
Zinc-Silver-Gold Alloys Obtained in the Cyanide Process.

CHAPTER IX.
Recovery of Silver from Nitrate Solutions.
The Precipitation of Chloride of Silver.
The reduction of Chloride.

CHAPTER X.
Refining by Means of Sulphuric Acid.
Experimental Work on Gold-Silver Alloys.
Experimental Work on Gold-Zinc Alloys.
Experimental Work on Gold-Zinc-Silver Alloys.
Experimental Work on Gold-Silver-Tellurium Alloys.
Parting with Sulphuric Acid Commercially.
The Gutzkow Process.
The Process as Carried on in Australia.

CHAPTER XI.
Parting Gold by Electrolysis—
Mobius' Process.
Description of the Plant.
The Improved Process.

CHAPTER XII.
Electrolytic Refining of Gold.
The Separation of Platinum from Gold.

CHAPTER XIII.
The Treatment of Cyanide Precipitates.
Gold Precipitated on Zinc.
The Clean-up of Zinc Slimes.
Smelting the Precipitate Direct.
Treatment with Sulphuric Acid.
Effect of Sand, Lead, and Other Impurities.
Removal of Lime and Lime Salts.
Experiments with Caustic Soda.
The Distillation Process.

CHAPTER XIV.
Other Methods of Refining Gold Slimes—
Treatment with Strong Nitric Acid.
Treatment with Strong Sulphuric Acid.
The Removal of Copper with Sulphuric Acid and Air.
Dissolving Out Gold with Chlorine.

CHAPTER XV.
The Nitre Cake Method of Purifying Slimes.
Experiments to Prevent Dusting.
The Manufacture of Nitre Cake.
The Direct Use of Nitre Cake.
Effect of Temperature.
Time Required.
Vessel Required.
Effect of Various Impurities.
Dry Method of Refining Slimes.
Caldecott's process.
Taverner's Process.
Merril's Process.
Slimes from Electro-refining of Copper.
Separation of Gold and Platinum.

Appendix—The Refining of Base Bullion.

PREFACE.

An effort has been made to present the essential points of all methods of gold refining commonly practised, as well as those of historic interest. No branch of metallurgy is older, yet the literature on the subject is so fragmentary and scattered that records of much valuable work have been lost sight of.

In spite of the fascination of the subject to workers in ancient and modern times, there is still scope for many special lines of research; it is the hope of the author that the work done in this direction during spare moments will be suggestive enough to stimulate others—and that such progress will be made, especially in the treatment of auriferous precipitates derived from the cyanide processes, that another edition will be necessary.

School of Mines,
Bendigo, June, '09.

GOLD REFINING.

CHAPTER I.

Introductory.—Gold, as it occurs in Nature, is never pure. Occasionally the amount of alloying metal is less than one per cent., but as a general rule it is greater; the commonest alloy, in fact, the invariable one, being composed of gold and silver. Sometimes traces of copper are present, but in all other instances elements such as iron and lead appear to be present as compounds admixed with the gold. Water is invariably present, large pieces giving as much as 0.5 per cent., while quartz and other admixtures are usually present in the cleanest specimens, and these will become at once apparent on fusing the gold in a porcelain crucible.

There is no difference in the same field between the gold to be found amongst the alluvium, or alluvial gold, and that existing in the quartz or other matrix. The gold occurring in the alluvium is not refined by any of Nature's processes—but the accompanying minerals or metals are either oxidised or removed—hence, in the recovery of gold from reefs impurities are often collected and introduced, thus making it of lower value than the corresponding alluvial gold, and also giving rise to erroneous and widespread statements to the contrary.

Alluvial gold in Australasia is, practically speaking, an alloy of gold and silver. In no place is its composition constant over any wide area, and perhaps the only general statements which can be made are that when it occurs in igneous rocks the percentage of silver is higher than in the sedimentary strata. In one shoot, or that portion of a reef which carries gold contents without any break, the ratio of gold to silver, so far as the writer's experience goes, is constant.

A.

Another shoot in the same reef may give slightly different values, but on the whole will approach the first, yet only a few feet away may occur a parallel reef with an altogether different ratio. To discover the natural solvents which carried gold and silver, and from which they were deposited in this constant alloy, would be to have at our disposal probably a new and effective method of refining base alloys.

Simple Methods of Purification. — The purification of such alluvial gold alloys is a simple matter. The high specific gravity of the metal allows of separation from most admixed materials by some process of elutriation, or water concentration, or, in arid regions, by dry blowing. The coarser particles are readily picked out, but the finer are usually admixed with heavy sands, consisting of crushed zircons, garnets, cassiterite, wolfram, titanite, menaccanite, and in fact, almost any heavy oxidised compound or mineral. In a few cases platinum and osmiridium also occur. The separation of the sand is effected either by fluxing it when melting the gold, or amalgamating the gold, and thereby separating it from the admixed sands. By smelting the gold freed from sand in a graphite pot with borax glass, the gold is obtained free from any metal, excepting traces, save silver. Should there be any oxides of heavy metals, such as oxide of tin, present the gold should be smelted in fireclay pots, so that these oxides may not be reduced, and the gold be contaminated with base metals.

There is no process for removing silver except in very small quantities from ordinary alluvial gold. Solvents only remove a film. If the alluvial gold be in thin flakes resembling bran, such gold being common in river beds, and far removed from the matrix of the gold, appreciable amounts of silver may be separated by a method to be hereafter described.

Refining of Gold Obtained by Other Processes. — (Amalgamated Gold.) — By far the greater portion of the gold won annually is obtained by amalgamation. Mercury is fed into stamper boxes or pans, so that it will have a chance of coming in contact with the gold as soon as the latter has been liberated by the crushing action of the stampers, or the grinding action of the pans. Mercury will first adhere to particles of gold, but in course of time penetrate them. Particles of amalgam adhere to each other, and in course of time every sheltered spot in the triturating appliances will serve as a resting place for the amalgam, which sometimes builds up into pieces weighing several pounds. Other metals also amalgamate; amongst these are native copper, also arsenic, antimony, bismuth, and some lead from compounds as well as silver compounds.

Pan Amalgamation. — In pan amalgamation such amalgamating action on the base metals is more pronounced than in a stamper box, mainly on account of the closer trituration of the metallic ores and the mercury, but also on account of the strong reducing action going on within the pan, finely divided iron and solutions re-acting giving rise to hydrogen gas, carburetted as well as arseniuretted hydrogen, all of which may be readily detected.

Copper Plate Amalgamation. — In addition to this a considerable quantity of amalgam is caught on copper plates, which have been amalgamated by giving them a coating of mercury. At first a copper amalgam forms, but after a short time, when running with auriferous ores, a film of gold silver amalgam forms—so long as copper amalgam lies on the surface of the plate, oxidation of the copper goes on, and a film of basic carbonate of copper forms, but as soon as the gold silver amalgam forms such oxidation ceases, and the plates remain bright. When amalgam is first collected from copper plates it is contaminated with copper, but subsequently, unless the copper has been scraped up, the amalgam formed will only contain a minute quantity of the base metal.

The impurities introduced by amalgamation processes thus depend on the quality of the ore, and the care taken to exclude amalgamable metals, although it is not possible to altogether exclude copper caps and fragments of brass, which become mixed with the ore from explosives used.

Purifying Mercury. — The first condition for obtaining pure bullion by amalgamation is to use pure mercury. Many methods have been recommended for this. They are based on the fact that impure mercury becomes covered with a film which either may be removed mechanically or chemically. One of the first methods is to shake the impure mercury with a little powdered sugar—the sugar will entangle the scum, and retain it—the mercury may be then run through a pin hole in a stout filter paper*.

Other methods are to oxidise or dissolve the impurities with dilute nitric acid, by allowing the mercury to trickle in a thin stream into the acid—the mercury is repeatedly agitated in order to bring any base metals into contact with the acid. Sometimes salts are used for the elimination of metals, for instance, ferric chloride solutions are used for the elimination of zinc or tin—the mercury in this case trickling into a deep vessel filled with a ferric chloride solution.

Methods of purification by retorting have also been proposed and carried out; one method consists in retorting with iron filings, the object of the iron filings being to remove the sulphur. This cannot be done at the temperature attained in retorting. Quicklime has also been recommended for the same purpose, and, finally, a layer of cinnabar, the object of which would be to form sulphides of the metals amalgamating with the mercury, the cinnabar itself being decomposed. This method is not free from objection, since arsenic or antimony are not removed, also the sulphide of mercury itself distils over. A simpler and more effective method proposed and carried out successfully by the writer is to place over the mercury a layer of some oxidising compound, and also alkaline compound, to unite with any volatile oxide which might form and thus retain it. Amongst such compounds are oxide of mercury and caustic potash, or nitrate of soda, nitrate of potash, or, better still, sodium peroxide. At a temperature approaching distillation these substances melt, and metals such as zinc are oxidised, and the oxide fixed as zincate of potash or soda. Arsenic, antimony, lead and sulphur, become respectively arseniate, antimoniate, plumbate and sulphate of sodium, while the non-volatile, heavy metals remain practically unaltered in the retort, or are partly oxidised.

Purifying Amalgam.—In spite of having pure mercury to start with, a number of impurities enter the gold

---

*Louis, p. 64, Handbook of Gold Milling.

silver amalgam in practice.   Some of these can be eliminated
by triturating the amalgam with mercury, so as to eliminate
any adhering impurities, then by immersing the amalgam in
mercury the gold-silver amalgam, if rich in gold, will sink,
and other amalgams will float.   The latter may be partly removed by skimming them off with a piece of sponge.   The
amalgam left should be squeezed through chamois leather or
calico, when mercury containing a small amount of amalgam
in solution passes through, and a gold silver amalgam remains.
Lead amalgam may be partly removed by heating the mercury
by means of steam, and squeezing the amalgam into warm
water; part of the lead amalgam passes through.

Refining Retorted Gold.—The amalgam so obtained
is retorted, and if the same plan is adopted with
regard to oxidising agents in this case as with mercury, the
base metals present with the gold will be for the most part
oxidised, while the mercury will distil away free from them.
The gold, if smelted in clay pots, needs only some borax flux
to dissolve the base metallic oxides.   The gold-silver alloy remaining is almost free from impurities, these being usually
less than three parts per thousand.   In ordinary practice this
precaution is not taken, but the retorted gold is broken up, and
melted in graphite crucibles.

CHAPTER II.

Refining with Oxidising and Chloridising Agents.

Nitre Refining.—When the molten gold is obviously
impure nitre is added, and as a rule its main action is to eat
the pot away, for as fast as metals are oxidised they are again
reduced by the carbon of the pots. Where fireclay crucibles
are used the nitre does effect a small amount of oxidation, but
the action is very imperfect, unless the bullion is very low
grade.   If the nitre is added before the retorted cakes have
commenced to melt, so that each honeycombed lump of gold is
penetrated by the fused salt, the action is much more perfect
than when it is thrown on the molten surface of gold. In some
cases where the alloy is brittle after melting, the slags from
the fluxes are thickened with bone-ash or other inert substance,
and are lifted off by means of a flat spiral of iron wire. This
is lowered on the surface of the slag, some slag is cooled, and
adheres. This is lifted out and pressed against a cold surface;
the slag now forms a circular cake adhering to the spiral; this
is again dipped down, raised and flattened, and the process
repeated until the molten metal surface becomes apparent.

Refining With Mercuric Chloride. — The temperature
is raised until the metals are high above their melting
points, when corrosive sublimate $Hg\ Cl_2$ is thrown in, and a
cover rapidly put on the pot. At a high temperature small
quantities of base metals which render bullion brittle are removed by this treatment, and the alloy or metal is toughened.
The process is only adapted for the removal of very small
quantities of antimony, arsenic, or elements having a high
atomic volume, and can not be recommended on account of the

poisonous fumes evolved in the process, for the bulk of the mercuric chloride is volatilised.

Refining with Ammonium Chloride. — Ammonium chloride is also used for the same purpose in the same manner. When thrown on the molten metal it gradually sublimes and dissociates. The hydrochloric acid evolved attacks the base metals and removes part of them. The process, however, is incomplete and ineffective in the presence of a large quantity of base metal. If solid ammonium chloride is pressed below the surface of molten gold, much spitting is occasioned. Another method sometimes adopted for toughening brittle gold does so by the introduction of copper, which replaces equivalents of other metals. In this case oxide of copper is added with the gold. This at a high temperature reacts with lead and other metals; the resulting bullion in this case, however, contains copper instead of the metals removed, and the process is a toughening one more than a refining one.

Refining with Iron. — Antimony and arsenic may be removed by stirring the molten metal with a bar of iron,[*] a little nitre being added at the same time. These elements unite with the iron to form antimonides or arsenides, but at the same time it must be borne in mind that iron itself dissolves in molten gold, so that it is not possible to hit upon the exact point at which the whole of the base metals will be removed, and the iron left undissolved by the gold.

Removal of Tin.—When tin is present carbonate of potassium is added, and heated with the molten metal.

Sometimes when nitre or other fusible corrosive refining agents or fluxes are used a layer of bone-ash is put over the surface of the molten bullion; small holes are made in this by scraping it to one side, and nitre or such fluxes added. When lead is present, sand and nitre are added.

Experimental Work. — For some years the author has endeavoured to devise a method for refining retorted gold. It was recognised that once the metal becomes melted the surface exposed to the action of refining agents is so small, and the latter decompose so rapidly, that only a small degree of purifi-

---

[*]Rose, Metallurgy of Gold, p. 389.

cation can be effected. With retorted gold, on the other hand, we have a porous material to deal with. The surface exposed is very large, and the refining fluxes are acting while the temperature is rising to melting point. The oxidation method with nitre and similar fluxes already described serves to cut out almost every metal save gold and silver. These cannot be used effectively in a plumbago pot, and clay pots are apt to become eaten through by the corroding action of the fluxes.

Refining with Sodium Bisulphate. — It was considered that the silver as well as the base metals might be removed by some preliminary treatment. Nitric acid was ineffective on the retorted gold tried; sulphuric acid had little effect, but on testing with bisulphate of sodium it was found that base metals were removed or oxidised, and that silver sulphate formed. The retorted gold was heated in porcelain or dense fireclay pots to a dull red heat for some time, generally as long as sulphur dioxide was evolved. The fused pyrosulphate was then poured out, and the cake drained as completely as possible. These were afterwards washed with hot water until the silver sulphate had been removed. The cake of melted pyrosulphate was also dissolved, and the silver present in the solution precipitated on iron, or by other well-known means. The gold could now be smelted, and invariably would be found to be much purer than when smelted by older methods. The silver and base metals were also removed at a fraction of the cost required by the chlorine method. The results obtained, however, were variable; one sample would be purified from about 80 to 96 per cent., yet another would only be increased by five or six per cent. The cause of this variation seemed to be that when coarse gold is amalgamated the mercury only affects the outer crust, so that on retorting there would be left pieces of gold porous on the outside, but unaltered within. In order to determine whether the gold and silver, if amalgamated in a fine state of division and then retorted would part, 80 grains of gold and 20 grains of silver were taken and amalgamated. The amalgam was retorted, and the resulting gold was of pale yellow colour. This was treated by boiling with strong sulphuric acid, which removed part of the silver; it was afterwards treated by fusion with sodium bisulphate, which removed more. The gold remaining was then washed with water, and after the silver sulphate had been removed the metal was weighed and parted. It was found to consist of: Gold, 97.2; silver, 2.8.

It is, therefore, a difficult matter to remove the whole of the silver, even when finely divided originally by this treatment. It might be stated here, although detailed reference will be made to it later on, that by using phosphoric acid with sulphate of sodium as a solvent that the retorted gold made in the same way was raised to

99.2 gold.

0.8 silver.

Refining with Sulphate of Silver and Salt.—These results were so promising that efforts were directed to shorten the process. The sulphate of silver takes a considerable time to wash out, and although the retorted gold is honeycombed, yet solution is retarded; and if any sulphate of silver remains it is decomposed on melting the bullion, and the silver becomes again alloyed with the gold.

If chloride of sodium is melted with sulphate of silver double decomposition takes place.

$$Ag_2SO_4 + 2NaCl = Na_2SO_4 + 2AgCl.$$

The resulting silver chloride is not decomposed at a high temperature, and is not sensibly volatile when protected by a layer of fused salt. By melting the bisulphate with the retorted gold, and pouring any excess out, and then adding salt, and melting in a clay pot, the resulting bullion becomes almost as pure as if prolonged washing were given to remove the soluble silver salt.

A modification of this process consisted in first heating the retorted gold with molten common salt, so that the pores became filled with it. The crucible was then closed with a cover, and bisulphate of sodium dissolved in strong sulphuric acid allowed to drop in gradually. The sulphur trioxide and hydrochloric acid, both of which attack silver at a high temperature, had to escape through the retorted mass of gold. As soon as it was considered the salt was decomposed more salt was added to convert any sulphate of silver to chloride, and the whole melted down. The result of this treatment,

so far as the refining was concerned, was satisfactory, but the
bubbling in the pot, due to decomposition of salt, and evolution of hydrochloric acid are objectionable features.   This
modification gave purer gold than the bisulphate method.

Refining with Boric and Phosphoric Acid.—It was
then considered that if some relatively non-volatile
acid were employed whose salts with silver were stable at a
high temperature that these might be used in place of chloride
of silver. The two which suggested themselves were boric and
phosphoric acids. In order to try if the salts would decompose
sulphate of silver, a mixture of sulphate of silver and boric
acid were heated gradually, and then up to the melting point
of gold. Sulphate of silver melted and decomposed, leaving
metallic silver at a red heat, but both the borate and phosphate
of silver which formed melted down and remained undecom-
posed at a temperature above the melting point of silver.
Borax has commonly been used as a refining agent, but so far
as I am aware, phosphoric oxide or acid has not.   Indeed
Percy goes so far as to say that "the phosphates of silver
have no metallurgical interest."[*]

A strip of thin silver was then placed in boric acid, which
was heated to redness; very slight action took place; when
oxide of silver was substituted the oxide dissolved up and
formed an opalescent mass, which was soluble in water, but
from which a small quantity of black powder separated. The
experiment was repeated with phosphoric acid. At a dull red
heat the silver was attacked, and bubbles of gas were evolved.
At a red heat no further action seemed to take place; the
liquid remained clear when molten, but on cooling the mass
solidified and turned black, when exposed to daylight. In this
case the metaphosphoric acid probably decomposed to a slight
extent into phosphoric oxide and water.   The boric acid
$B_2O_3 3H_2O$ at 100 deg. C. becomes $B_2O_3 2H_2O$, and at 140
deg. C. $B_2O_3 H_2O$, and at a high temperature B_2O_3.   It is
probable that while H_2O is present the oxygen necessary for
the formation of the borate is supplied, but the action ceases
when this is expelled. .

[*]Percy, Gold and Silver, p. 139.

Phosphoric Acid and Oxidising Agents. — Knowing that molten silver readily absorbs oxygen experiments were conducted to see if the addition of oxygen to alloys of gold and silver surrounded by phosphoric acid or boric acid would remove it. The first method thought of was by bubbling oxygen through the molten alloy, and having a cover of these acids, but it was considered that by heating weighed beads before the blowpipe in an oxidising flame that quicker results could be attained.

Boric Acid and Oxidising Agents.—A boric acid bead was made on platinum wire, and an alloy of gold containing 72.14 per cent. of gold was used. The alloy taken weighed 0.192 grains. It was melted carefully, and the bead heated strongly in an oxidising blast. After about five minutes the bead, on cooling, became an opalescent grey colour, due to the oxide of silver dissolving in the boric acid. The bead weighed 0.188 grains. On re-heating for another five minutes the weight became 0.186 grains. Further heating for the same time did not reduce the weight appreciably. The weight of the silver was thus reduced by 11 per cent., but it does not seem possible to remove all the silver by this means.

Phosphoric Acid and Oxidising Agents. — In the next experiment micro-cosmic salt [H Na NH$_4$ PO$_4$] was used instead of phosphoric acid, since it has the same effect, and is not so fluid when melted as the latter, thus retaining the gold bead better. The same alloy was used, and 0.3 grains taken. On heating in the oxidising flame the bead became opalescent very quickly, and after five minutes the button weighed 0.290. Previous experiments had shown that it was somewhat difficult to keep the bead from running up and alloying with the platinum, so the bead was transferred to a small dish in which the flux was placed, and the bead heated as before in the oxidising flame. After the second fusion it weighed 0.280; after the third 0.270; after the fourth 0.263; after the fifth 0.258; the sixth 0.253; the seventh 0.250; the eighth 0.249. As the loss seemed to be approaching a limit a fine drop of sulphuric acid was added to the flux to determine the effect. The weight was reduced to 0.243; with another drop on re-melting the weight became 0.235, but after

this the loss became very slight, only reaching 0.231. It is
needless to state the button passed from a very pale to a bright
yellow colour. The gold has been raised from 72.14 per cent.
to 93.5 per cent., and 82 per cent. of the silver slagged off.
This experiment shows that phosphoric acid in conjunction
with oxygen, or an oxidising agent, has a powerful effect
in tending to remove silver from gold. It was considered that
the sulphuric acid formed hydrogen sodium sulphate, and
liberated phosphoric acid in the cold, but on heating the non-
volatility of the phosphoric acid would result in the expulsion
of sulphur trioxide, and this would serve to attack the silver,
but the second change would result in a relative stable phosphate of silver and sodium being formed.

In order to test the effect on a somewhat larger scale a
piece of retorted gold was taken. The weight of this was 243
grains, and the amount of gold the button contained, as tested
by another sample, on melting was 86.4 per cent., the balance
being nearly all silver. The retorted gold was placed in a
porcelain dish, and 5 grammes of sodium bisulphate melted with
it. After cooling a saturated solution of phosphoric acid was
added, and the water driven off, and the whole placed in a
muffle and left for some hours at a red heat. Bubbles of gas
were freely evolved from the cake, and a clear, greenish,
fusible slag remained. The gold was picked out, and the slag
allowed to drain away from it. On being placed in water it
gave a solution which reacted for silver. The slag, however,
was not wholly dissolved out, but the cake was put in a French
clay crucible, and melted down; a bright gold button weighing
215 grains was obtained. This assayed 977 fine gold; the
balance being silver only.

Another experiment was made on a very base sample of
retorted gold from Dargo (V.), which contained mainly gold,
silver and copper. This was treated as in the previous case;
the slag in this case, however, was turquoise blue. On melting
down the button obtained an attempt was made to pour the
small quantity of slag left in the pot, but the gold had not
quite solidified, and ran down the side of the pot. When the
small bar was taken out it was almost as white as silver.
This coat proved to be merely superficial, and may have re-

sulted from a fragment of reducing agent passing into the slag at the last moment, although a similar superficial white film can often be seen on pouring a high-grade gold bullion which has been melted under nitre. The weight of the retorted gold received, which was greenish-black in colour, was 322 grains.

When refined, 221 grains.
It assayed: gold, 98.15 per cent.
        silver, 1.73
oxidisable metals, 0.12.

These examples serve to show that phosphoric acid might be made use of with great advantage in the purification of retorted base bullion. It is better than boracic acid or borax in not dissolving silica, and, therefore, it does not corrode the crucibles; it forms a readily fusible slag, capable of dissolving basic oxides, and if made use of after the manner indicated, it will remove a large quantity of silver from the retorted gold as well as base metals. There is no loss of gold by volatility through its action, and the silver can readily be reduced from the slags containing it by the action of iron in a slightly acid solution, or by the reducing action of suitable fluxes.

The small amount of silver remaining in the gold can be removed by the action of a current of chlorine being passed through the molten metal. It is also possible that some classes of retorted gold will yield a bullion over 995 fine.

Refining with Potassium Chlorate. — In addition to these methods, chlorate of potash was tried, by melting it on retorted gold, so as to allow it to soak into the cake. The oxygen evolved served to oxidise base metals; by adding some relatively fixed acid, such as is evolved from sodium pyrosulphate, chlorine is evolved. This serves to give a high-grade bullion, but the method was discarded when it was found that chloride of gold was carried away with the escaping vapours or gases evolved. Other oxygen carriers, such as chromates and manganates, were added, but the results were no better than those already described.

CHAPTER III.

Sulphur Refining.

Refining with Sulphur. — A more speedy method of removing iron, copper, lead and base metals from bullion is to add sulphur to the molten metals.

Although gold sulphides may be readily formed in the wet way, they are decomposed into gold and sulphur by merely heating them to a temperature below 300 deg. C. If pure gold is heated strongly with sulphur no combination of the elements appears to take place. Nearly all the other metals at a bright red heat unite readily with sulphur, and form sulphides. If a large proportion of copper be alloyed with gold then by granulating the alloy and heating gradually in a graphite pot a sulphide of copper or matte will readily form, and if the temperature is raised to melt the gold a button of gold containing up to 96 per cent., or even more, of the metal may be obtained. If attempts are made to convert the whole of the copper into a sulphide a large proportion of the gold will remain diffused through the copper matte, mainly in a finely divided condition, although part exists as a double sulphide of gold and copper. When silver is present as well as gold part of the silver passes into the matte as sulphide, but it is almost impossible to remove the whole of the silver from the gold button. When it is desired to add sulphur to an impure molten mixture of gold and base metals, the sulphur is sprinkled round the edge of the molten mass to prevent spitting, as would otherwise be the case if it were added at the centre.

The objection to adding sulphur in this way is that as soon as the sulphides form they float on the surface, so that any additional quantity added only volatilises unchanged. A better method was suggested by Mr. Manton, of Kalgoorlie. By melting the bullion first, and then having a smaller pot filled with sulphur, and inverting this into the molten mass, the sulphur vapour forces the metal as fast as it is formed from underneath the inverted pot to the space between the outer and inner pots. This method is open to the objection that the inverted pot chills and solidifies a crust of gold; the amount of sulphur which can be used with safety in this way is small, and there is danger of a violent volatilisation of the sulphur projecting the molten material out of the pot. By modifying the process in providing a means for a steady supply of sulphur into the inverted pot until the action is complete this method is one of the simplest and the most effective in cutting out most base metals from gold.

When the action has gone as far as desired it is better to allow the gold to solidify in the pot, most of the matte can then be poured off from the solid gold. If the matte also is allowed to solidify the crucible may be inverted, and the gold and matte dropped out. The matte, as a rule, can be knocked off. If the gold and matte are poured into a mould there is often the greatest difficulty in separating them. A complex matte, consisting as it often does of gold, silver, antimony, copper, and iron sulphides, clings persistently to the gold bar, and is not appreciably attacked by nitre or sulphuric acid. It is often noted that such impure bars sink very much in the centre on cooling; the matte runs in and fills up this longitudinal depression, making it still more difficult to get out. In order to remove this material probably the simplest way is to heat the bar to redness and sprinkle nitre on the matte until it ceases to glow. It is thereby loosened owing to the formation of sulphates, and may be more readily removed. By repeating the operation the gold bar may be rendered superficially clean.

While very impure bullion may be partly purified in this way very readily, yet it is not possible to remove appreciable amounts of silver and copper from ordinary alluvial or retorted bullion by this means. In other words, bullion containing only 10 per cent. of gold can readily be brought up to 90 per cent., but if the latter is taken, it is more difficult to raise it to 95 per cent. than to carry out the first separation.

The gold and silver present in the matte may be separated by adding some finely divided copper oxide, or even stirring round with an iron rod; portion of the copper sulphide is transformed to copper, which collects the gold and silver present into a button.

Refining with Sulphur and other Metals Conjointly. —The process of separating gold from silver and other metals by means of sulphur has been known for centuries, and has been fully described by Percy. * It was commonly used up to the 18th century, and even now there are many important technical operations which the modern metallurgist should be acquainted with.

The first process described is by Theophilus, written in the eleventh century. The gold-silver alloy was granulated; a portion of the granulations was heated with sulphur at a low temperature. The sulphur formed sulphide of silver and melted. The gold for the most part remained intermixed, or even in solution in this molten mass. In order to precipitate it a further addition of the granulated alloy was added. This collected and precipitated the gold. The mass was heated strongly, allowed to cool in the pot; when cold the pot was inverted, and the solidified mass emptied out. The sulphide was separated from the metal by the blow of a chisel applied at the junction of metal and sulphide. The alloy, now very much enriched in gold, was cupelled with lead in order to separate the sulphides, and clean the metal. The resulting alloy was parted with nitric acid. The sulphides broken off were mixed with lead and cupelled. The silver, still containing a little gold, being thus recovered.

A modification of this process was to granulate the alloy; moisten it so as to cause the sulphur, which was mixed with the granules, to adhere more closely; to heat gently, and then more strongly, forming sulphide of silver. A small amount of iron was then added, or the mixture stirred with an iron rod, and the gold and portion of the silver was thereby collected. The separation of the gold and silver by means of litharge, cupellation, and nitric acid were the same as in the former example.

Another modification of these processes after the granu-

*Percy's Metallurgy, Gold and Silver, Vol. I., p. 356.

lated alloy has been melted with sulphur, litharge is sprinkled so that the reduced silver will carry down the gold.

$$2PbO + 3Ag_2 S = 2PbS + 6Ag + SO_2.$$

Some lead is simultaneously reduced and alloyed with the gold and silver.

This operation has to be repeated until the silver sulphide is free from gold. The precipitated alloy after cupellation was treated with nitric acid. The regulus or mixed sulphides is melted with scrap iron to precipitate the silver and lead. The alloy was cupelled, and the iron sulphide sent to the blast furnace.

These methods, depending on the separation of gold from silver, were only applicable as concentrating processes. No attempt appears to have been made to obtain fine gold by this method of treatment. From experiments made by the author on granulated alloys, also very fine alluvial gold, having a high ratio of gold-silver; very little silver is removed from such alloys by means of sulphur alone. The gold present in the sulphides, such as sulphide of silver, sulphide of copper, sulphide of iron, appears to be in the state of a sulphide also, or else it is in solution, while these are molten, and remains disseminated when the sulphides are cooled.

On heating about 50oz. of auriferous copper scalings with sulphur, and melting at a high temperature, only a small proportion of the gold separated in the form of a button. On re-melting with more copper scale practically the whole of the gold was precipitated, and this gold contained very little copper. This would indicate that the gold was in the form of a sulphide, and was displaced by the copper. On the other hand, when the rich auriferous regulus was broken, bright scales like gold could be seen. This apparent separation of gold may, however, have taken place on cooling in the same manner as metallic copper will separate in moss-like form from copper matte on cooling; similarly metallic silver will separate in spongy, or hair-like forms from sulphide of silver formed as indicated in the preceding cases, when the mass becomes cold.

On dissolving such mattes in nitric acid, part of the gold sometimes appears as if it were unaltered, and had not combined with the associated elements, but on the other hand

B

sometimes the whole of it is obtained as a brown, spongy mass such as is left when gold compounds or gold alloys are acted upon by acids such as nitric. It would therefore appear that although gold sulphide is readily decomposed at a moderate temperature into gold and sulphur, that when it is intermixed with other sulphides containing excess of sulphur that it dissolves in them, and that, on cooling, part of it is rejected as metallic gold, but part remains either as metal in a solidified solution or as a sulphide.

Refining with Sulphur and Sodium. — From experimental work done, the author was driven to the conclusion that a carrier is needed for the sulphur and silver alloyed with gold. The effect of sulphur itself is transient when its vapour comes in contact with molten gold containing silver. If it were forced through the molten alloy its effect would be more marked, but it is doubtful if it will quantitatively remove the silver from the gold. Since its action is more effective when metals having a great affinity for it are present, an experiment was tried with metallic sodium and gold, to which sulphur was added. The alloy of sodium, silver and gold is very liquid at a low temperature. The formation of the alloy was first attempted by melting the gold with sodium in a cavity scooped out of a charcoal block, but the alloy formed was so fluid as to soak into the pores of the charcoal. Alloys were subsequently made in hard glass tubes, or in porcelain crucibles enclosed in plumbago ones. By heating gradually, with exclusion of air, the gold rapidly dissolved in a comparatively small weight of sodium, and formed a uniform alloy. On adding sulphur to this alloy the sulphur united with the metals with great vigour, raising them to a very high temperature.

The first qualitative experiments showed that silver could be removed by this method as well as base metals, and quantitative tests were made to see what actually took place when the alloy was subjected to this treatment. An alloy consisting of

      72.14 gold
      27.82 silver
       0.04 copper

was taken and mixed with sodium in the proportion of 10 to 1, or 10 grammes of the alloy and one gramme sodium.

The mixture was placed in a porcelain crucible, which was put in a clay crucible, a large porcelain lid of a crucible was inserted into the clay pot, leaving ample room between it and the top of the porcelain crucible. When the pot became red hot small pieces of sulphur were dropped on the porcelain lid. They rapidly melted and trickled down into the lowest compartment, thereby coming in contact with the molten alloy. When the pot had been raised to a full red heat it was withdrawn from the fire and allowed to cool. The porcelain crucible was lifted out, and placed in water and boiled. At first a strong yellow solution formed, with a few black specks through it. This was filtered, and the filtrate kept. Fresh water was added, and the metal and matte boiled until nothing more dissolved. The fused mass became detached from the crucible, and consisted of a button of gold below and a dark, waxy-looking layer above. The upper surface of the latter had a film of gold, no doubt due to some air getting access to the crucible on cooling. The gold button was detached and weighed. Its weight was 3.25 grms. It consisted of gold and silver in the following proportions:

gold, 87.1
silver, 12.9.

The standard had, therefore, been raised about 15 per cent., but instead of having 7.21 grms. of fine gold there was only 2.83 grms., the balance having passed into the matte. Again it would be thought that the gold from this would have been precipitated by the free silver still present in the button. This may possibly be the case if the mixture is kept molten for a considerable time, for previous experiments indicated that a higher grade gold can be obtained by this means, and a smaller proportion passed into the matte.

To the solution from the matte dilute sulphuric acid was added until it was acid. At first a port wine colour formed, but on adding more acid, a brown precipitate fell, and sulphuretted hydrogen was evolved, after a little time a white precipitate of sulphur came down—the precipitate was filtered, dried and heated, and was found to consist of sulphide of gold. The weight of gold obtained from this was 0.431grms., this was 992 fine. The weight of pure gold was, therefore, 0.4275grms. The remainder was silver.

The sulphide matte remaining after washing weighed 6.97 grammes. On being broken the matte had a columnar fracture. It was examined with a glass, but no gold could be seen in it save the film before mentioned. The matte was gently washed in a porcelain crucible. Strong sulphuric acid, and subsequently bisulphate of soda, were added, heated, washed, and the gold and silver collected separately.

After the fusion with bisulphate the gold hung together after the manner of retorted gold; it had the same apparently uniform external crust, and the same sponginess inside, and the same tenacity. In fact it was undistinguishable from it. After washing the silver out, the residue was smelted in a clay pot with phosphoric acid and a small quantity of bisulphate of soda. The resulting gold assayed 996, and weighed 3.92 grammes. The slag resulting from this fusion was a magnificent ruby color by reflected light, and some of it this color by transmitted light, and some a rich violet blue, resembling very much solutions from which gold has been precipitated. It contains a small quantity of gold, which probably gave the color to it. A summary of the forms in which the gold existed is as follows:—

Gold in melted button 2.831
Gold in the matte 3.904
Gold soluble in water .. .. .427

Total .. .. 7.162 grms.

The amount originally present was 7.21grms., so that 0.05 grms. are not accounted for here. On testing the silver obtained from the matte it was found to contain a minute proportion of gold, there was also gold left in the slag, and when sulphur was added to the gold sodium alloy sparks were evolved, so that some would thus escape treatment.

Sulphide of gold, soluble in water containing sodium

sulphide, always appears to carry a little silver through with it, since the gold obtained after cupellation is not fine.

In view of the readiness with which sulphur, in conjunction with sodium, would attack gold and silver, it seems a roundabout way of making the material, when sulphide of sodium with excess of sulphur might be added itself to the molten alloys, yet experiments made on these lines gave no results at all like the previous one. The gold and the silver remained almost unattacked when melted with sulphide of sodium to which sulphur was from time to time added. Several more crucial experiments were made by taking cyanide slime precipitates containing 14 per cent. of gold in a fine state of division. These were heated with sulphide of sodium, anhydrous thiosulphate of sodium, and polysulphide of sodium. In each case five grammes of slimes was taken, and 5, 10, 15 grammes of the sulphur compound. They were heated in a closed crucible to redness, and then washed with water. The solution was acidified, a precipitate of sulphur formed H_2S was given off. The precipitate was dried carefully, burned, and wrapped in sheet lead and cupelled. In no case was there more than a trace of gold in solution, and accompanying it was as much silver. The proportion of gold dissolved could be accounted for by the action of thiosulphate of sodium which forms when the solution of alkaline sulphides are brought into contact with the air. These results surprised me, since it has generally been accepted that gold is readily soluble in fused alkaline sulphides. Time did not permit of following out this line of investigation, but the subject will be dealt with more fully later on.

As far as researches have gone at present it seems necessary to have an alloy with the gold which has a great affinity for sulphur, in order to remove the silver in the state of sulphide. The alloying metal acts as a carrier of sulphur throughout the mass of molten metal. It may be that other investigators found that the alkaline sulphides attacked gold by actually reducing some sodium compound to metallic sodium in contact with gold; this would alloy with the gold, and if sulphur was present at the same time the effect would be the same as described on adding sulphur to a prepared alloy.

Refining by Means of Sulphide of Antimony.—
This process is also some centuries old, and is based
on the fact that when gold-silver alloys are melted with
sulphide of antimony sulphide of silver will form, and the gold
will alloy with the antimony.

$$Au + 6Ag + Sb_2S_3 = Au + 2Sb + 3Ag_2S$$

Copper and other metals will also be removed by this process.

It differs from the method of refining by sulphur alone
in that high grade bullion can be taken and refined to more
than 99.3 per cent. gold. Percy (p. 367, Gold and Silver, vol.
I.) states:—"It is sulphur that is really the agent by which
silver is separated from gold in this process; but, as it is in
combination with antimony, it may be kept in contact with
the alloy of those metals at a much higher temperature than
is practically possible when it is uncombined, the presence
of antimony not interfering, because it has a less affinity than
silver for sulphur." Since the heat formation of antimony
sulphide is 34 ($Sb_2 S_3$), and of silver sulphide ($Ag_2 S$) is 0.3
or 3 $Ag_2 S = 9$, the explanation given is not complete.
The affinity of gold for antimony, and the high temperature
must also be taken into account. The influence of mass has
also to be considered, for it is not possible to carry on this
operation with the equivalent of sulphur necessary for the
silver.

The quantity of sulphide of antimony to be added
depends on the amount of silver present, and the amount of
base metal, such as copper. This amount varies from twice
in the case of high grade bullion, to four times in the case of
baser bullion. The alloy is first melted, and then sulphide of
antimony is added. The crucible should not be more than two-
thirds full on account of the danger of frothing over. As
soon as sparks are emitted, the mass is poured, and the
sulphide detached from the gold antimony alloy, which still
contains silver. The latter is again melted with an additional
quantity of stibnite equal to twice the weight of the alloy;
finally the operation is repeated with an equal weight of
antimony sulphide. The operation is repeated if necessary
until the gold is of the desired standard. Some of the gold

remains in the fused sulphide. This is separated by fusing the latter for a considerable time, when the gold alloyed with silver separates. This button is treated in the same manner as the bullion. The antimony is separated from the gold by blowing a current of air over the surface of the molten metal. As the antimony is removed the melting point rises, and at the finish nitre and borax are added to remove the oxides and give a clear surface to the molten gold. The sulphides are treated by melting them with lead and iron. The resulting lead is cupelled, and the silver obtained is parted with nitric acid; the sulphide of antimony and iron have to be further treated to extract the silver still contained. This process was in use up to 1846, but is too costly as compared with the sulphuric process, or the Miller process of refining high grade bullion. There are also too many operations in the process, too many by-products, and the gold is not wholly separated from the silver in the final matte, nor is the silver from the gold in the final gold product.

Not only will sulphur serve for the separation of silver from gold when much silver is present, but other sulphides with the addition of sulphur also serve the same purpose. Sulphide of copper, for example, with sulphur will remove a considerable part of silver from gold, but the operation must be repeated several times in order to obtain gold of high standard. In this case also the gold-silver should be melted with copper, if it is not present already, the alloy granulated and the granules moistened, mixed with sulphur as before, and the whole mixture heated gradually but finally to a high temperature. The matte is broken off and the operation repeated on the alloy, with, if necessary, the addition of more copper. A considerable amount of the gold also passes into the matte; this may be precipitated along with the silver by the addition of some iron.

There is no doubt that this method is the simplest for the treatment of the cupriferous bullion often obtained in cyanide precipitates.

CHAPTER IV.

Cementation Processes.

Older processes for separating silver from gold by cementation were carried on practically in two ways, the first by heating gold for a long time with a mixture which evolved nitric acid on heating, and an absorbent into which any fusible salts ran; the mixture in the second method contained common salt as an essential ingredient, and some material which would assist in giving off hydrochloric acid and chlorine, also an absorbent for the fusible salts which liquated out. Detailed historical accounts of these are supplied in Percy's Metallurgy,* and it will be sufficient to briefly outline the processes. The impure bullion was rolled into thin plates about $4\frac{1}{2}$ inches square. Each plate was then coated with a layer of nitrate of potash and clay, and these were packed one above the other. They were then surrounded by clean, dry cow dung, which was set on fire. Cow dung burns slowly and perfectly, leaving a white ash. The heat generated was sufficient to decompose the nitrate, which, in the presence of siliceous matter becomes silicate of potash, and the water evolved from the dehydration of the clay, combining with the oxides of nitrogen, forms nitric acid, which, in its turn, attacks the silver on the surface of the alloy, forming nitrate of silver. The nitrate of silver is absorbed by the burnt clay and is also decomposed, thus supplying more nitric acid. It is somewhat remarkable that although nitric acid will not attack such alloys as are so treated when they are immersed in it, yet in both cementation processes the silver is removed for a considerable

*Percy, Gold and Silver, p. 379.

depth. The increased temperature and the expansion of the alloy, and the diffusion of the particles, probably accounts for the attack of such solvents.

Generally three firings with cow dung were given, the ashes being removed from the sides of the pile each time, and the silver which had liquated out in the form of nitrate was recovered from them. After the three firings the plates were taken and washed with water—the burnt clay and adhering silver being removed. The operation of applying the mixture and repeating the firings was again performed. Each dressing and heating caused the removal of some silver, but it was not until six dressings and eighteen firings had been applied that the gold was considered pure. The silver from the clays and ashes was recovered by smelting with litharge and charcoal, and the resulting lead bullion cupelled.

The second process of cementation, or the formation of a cementing mass, was by means of common salt and brick dust. This mixture was heated in contact with thin gold-silver plates for a long time. The action of the salt on the clay, together with the oxygen of the air and watery vapor, resulted in the formation of silicate of sodium, hydrochloric acid and chlorine. The result was that the chlorine compound attacked the silver, converting it into chloride, which was absorbed by the cementing medium.

Many modifications of this ancient method of refining were in use, such as the addition of ferrous and cupric sulphates to the chloride mixtures, and the addition of ammonium chloride, but the final action was invariably due to chlorine or hydrochloric acid. As a modification of the method of applying the mixture to gold in the form of plates, it was sometimes granulated, but the granules must have offered more difficulty in the separation of the gold from the adhering cementing mixture.

As in the case of nitric acid the alloys of gold and silver are acted upon by this cementing mixture, while if the plates themselves were immersed in hot hydrochloric acid they would be only superficially acted upon. There seems to be no doubt that diffusion plays a very important part in these cementation processes—not only of the gaseous products through or

into the plates, which was looked upon as the sole reason
of the formation of the silver compounds, but the actual
transfusion of the metals themselves at a slightly elevated
temperature.   For instance, if an alloy of gold and silver,
which is white on melting, be rendered gold-colored by having
the silver superficially removed by a suitable solvent, be
heated, it will become white.   The superficial golden layer
has been re-absorbed, although the temperature is far below
the melting point of the alloy.

The diffusion of carbon in iron far below its melting point
has been abundantly proved by Roberts Austin (Nature,
Vol. XLI, p. 14).   The chapter by the same author in his
Introduction to Metallurgy, 4th edition, pp. 56, 66, shows
that miscible solids diffuse through each other in a similar
manner to liquids.   Such diffusion is largely dependent on
temperature.   In the case of the gold-silver alloys, the
explanation of the cementation process is that a superficial
removal of silver occurs, the alloy is rendered poorer in this
metal and more diffuses from the interior; this in turn is
removed and the action goes on until very little remains.   It
naturally follows, the thinner the plate the more rapidly will
the silver be removed.   The term cementation has been
transferred to another class of operations, in which solid
elements are added to others by merely heating them in contact—for instance, the transference of carbon of metallic
iron by packing the latter in charcoal dust and heating; the
iron takes up carbon, and is thereby converted into steel;
probably the method of packing the metals suggested the
term, but in the case of steel the packing material does not
cement, nor does it withdraw anything from the iron, yet in
reality the action in both cases is due mainly to the diffusion
of solids in solids.

CHAPTER V.

Refining of Gold Bullion by Means of Oxygen or Air.

The method of removing oxidisable metals by means of an oxidising agent has been practised for centuries. The operation has already been described in the cementation process with nitre, and the gaseous method of removing antimony from gold. The ordinary cupellation operations are also on the same lines. When oxidising fluxes are used, their action is limited, since the oxygen they contain is rapidly evolved when brought into contact with gold at a high temperature—moreover, it only acts on a portion of the metal on the surface at the time. When air is allowed to pass, or is blown over molten metals a large surface must be exposed, as in a cupelling furnace, for the operation to be reasonably rapid.

In the year 1894 the author had to deal with considerable quantities of gold sent down from the Gippsland mines; much of the gold was exceedingly impure, and it was found that the action of ordinary refining fluxes, although good up to a certain point, never served to remove anything near the whole of the base metals present. Experiments were made by blowing air on to the surface of the molten metal, to promote oxidation, and removing the oxides by means of borax. This proved to be too slow. Air was then blown into the molten mass, but although it appeared to act rapidly, there was difficulty in keeping the pressure constant. As a result, on two occasions the gold was projected out of the pot, and the trouble of collecting it out of the coke and ashes was not compensated by the results obtained. For small amounts, the method took up too much time, and required too much atten-

tion to be persevered with.   Had a cylinder of oxygen been
available, this would have been tried, instead of air; but so
far as experiments went at the time, it appeared that the
process, while it would serve for the oxidation of impurities,
yet would be attended with so much spitting, or projection of
fine particles of gold, as to be practically of no value.   This
opinion was expressed in discussing this question in 1901.[*]
Dr. Kirk Rose[†] in 1904 ably deals with this subject.   Oxygen
from cylinders was allowed to escape through composition
pipes of about $\frac{1}{8}$ inch bore to a clay pipe dipping to the bottom
of the pot.   The connections were made of rubber tubing,
fastened on with rubber solution.   The pipes used were those
made for the Miller chlorine process.   They are made of clay,
about $\frac{1}{8}$ inch bore.   The oxides formed corroded them
quickly at the mouth of the pipe at the beginning of the
experiment.   When air was used it had little effect on the
pipes.

The stream of gas was regulated by a screw clip just above
the crucible; a small stream was turned on, and the pipe
slowly heated in the furnace, and then gradually inserted into
the molten metal.   The passage of the gas could be felt by
the throbbing of the rubber tube.   Dr. Rose took the
precaution to cover his crucible, so that any projected shots
of gold would be saved.

The molten metal was covered with sand and borax, so
that the oxides of the base metals might form a fluid
slag, without undue attack on the pot.   The amount of sand
added was calculated to provide a fluid slag on the completion
of the experiment.

The pots used were made of plumbago, with a fireclay
lining.   The graphite in a plumbago pot would undo the work
of the oxygen.

Dr. Rose first studied the effect produced when oxygen is
blown through molten metals or alloys, and compounds of
these, and refers specially to the refining of such low grade
gold bullion as is frequently produced from zinc boxes in

---

*Refining Gold Bullion with Oxygen Gas, Institute of M. and Met.,
Vol. XIV.
†" Australian Mining Standard."

the cyanide process. The effect of blowing oxygen through molten gold would result in the retention of part of the oxygen, and if an acid slag were present there would probably be formed a silicate of gold. The amount, however, under the conditions necessary for refining would be insignificant. Silver, on the other hand, absorbs large quantities of oxygen, when melted in the air it absorbs about 20 times its volume, or 0.27 per cent. by weight. This would correspond to 3.64 per cent. of silver oxide. By the law of partial pressures, much more should be dissolved, if it is a matter of mere solution, in oxygen. If at a high temperature, in presence of an acid slag, such as borax or silica, the silver in the form of oxide, unites with these materials, and passes into the slag as a borate or silicate. This was abundantly proved by experiment. Copper, lead, nickel, iron and zinc are readily oxidised when molten by a stream of oxygen, and if a suitable acid flux is provided the oxides of these metals will readily form silicates at the moment of conversion.

Tellurium and selenium pass off at a high temperature as oxides, unless the metal containing them is covered with slag, in which case they are retained to a greater or less extent. Antimony behaves similarly.

Dr. Rose believes that platinum, palladium, rhodium, iridium could be oxidised by this method at a high temperature and slagged off, although it is possible that some of them would be partly protected by silver.

Some important conclusions are arrived at, which tend to alter the current belief on the cause of the removal of base metals from bullion by oxidisation. It is well known that cuprous oxide forms when copper is melted in contact with air. The cuprous oxide remains dissolved in the molten metal. If the mass is allowed to solidify, this oxide separates out and remains scattered through the mass in small particles. If a large quantity forms, over 9 per cent. of Cu_2O, then the excess rises to the surface, and can be slagged off. The cuprous oxide is therefore a carrier of oxygen to more oxidisable metals.

Silver in the same way probably absorbs oxygen, and becomes silver oxide Ag_2O, and on passing a current of

oxygen through molten silver, silver oxide can be slagged off
if borax is over the surface. It can easily be seen that if
iron, nickel, lead, and other oxidisable metals are present, that
oxygen will be supplied to them by these oxygen carriers, and
the visible effect will be that they are transformed into oxides.

$$Cu_2O + Fe = 2Cu + FeO.$$
$$Ag_2O + Pb = 2Ag + PbO.$$

While an excess of base metals is present, the silver oxide is
reduced as fast as it is formed, but towards the finish of the
operation silver oxide is carried away. One notable result
is that while most of the base metals are oxidised by silver
oxide, and the silver reduced thereby, forming protective
agents against slagging off of silver, yet copper does not exert
this protective influence; in other words, much silver can be
removed by an oxidising process into the slag, while part of
the copper still remains in the bullion.

Generally speaking, the metals are oxidised successively,
each acting as a protective agent for the other; the order of
their removal is not sharply defined, but is in general accordance with their heat formations, zinc being first eliminated.

Heat of Combination with
16gms. of Oxygen.

Large calories (K)

Zinc to ZnO	827
Iron to Fe_2O_3	637
Lead to PbO	503
Nickel to Ni_2O_3	401
Copper to Cu_2O—less than	372
Platinum to PtO	179
Silver to Ag_2O	59
Gold to Au_2O—not more than ..	44
Antimony to Sb_2O_3	553
Arsenic to As_2O_3	516
Carbon to CO_2	471
Bismuth to Bi_2O_3	460
Tellurium to TeO_2	386
Sulphur to SO_2 .. ..:	346

The slag making material used consisted of borax and sand; the former was found to be too corrosive, but a suitable admixture of the two, mainly depending on the amount or bases present, will give a fluid and non-corrosive slag. The general formula given is $3(Na_2O. B_2O_3 + 6RO) + (B_2O_3)\ 3SiO_2$, where $R = Ca, Mg, Pb, Zn, Cu, Sb, \frac{2}{3}Fe, \frac{2}{3}Ni$.

The shots of gold can be recovered from the slag by concentration, and the silver and the balance of the gold by melting with iron and carbon.

By using air instead of oxygen the operation was much simpler, and required very little attention. Practically the only cost would be in keeping the metals melted while the operation was proceeding, and if this were done in a gas-heated furnace, holding a number of pots, it would be much cheaper than most of the processes now in operation.

At the time Dr. Rose wrote his paper he was not aware of any work having been done on the subject at all, but it subsequently transpired that this method of refining crude bullion was actually practised at Menzies, in W.A., and a patent for it taken out in 1896 by Messrs. Manton and Rayfield. In January, 1906, I learnt that experimental work was done at the Great Boulder mine on a large scale. A conical cast-iron pot, shaped like a slag pot, was lined with fire bricks and heated by means of a charcoal fire. The bullion was melted in a Faber du Faur furnace, and about 6000oz. poured into the converter. Unfortunately the slag from the melted gold was not first eliminated, and this on entering the converter attacked the ashes and charcoal remaining and boiled over. The clay pipes provided for forcing the air in also gave trouble, and the experiment failed for want of attention to preliminary detail. It was said to be very successful on a small scale. but lead was usually added to help to slag off the copper as oxide.

The method of refining by means of oxygen gas or air has advantages for certain grades of bullion. The methods at present available are cupellation and treatment by chlorine gas. The former involves some expense in erection and maintenance, and bye-products have to be worked up. The latter is expensive in operation, and noxious fumes are evolved.

The natural places for the development of the oxygen refining process are the mints and refining establishments. In spite of the comparative ease with which it can be worked by those accustomed to handling and melting metals, there would be much danger of loss in most small works if this process were generally introduced. These losses would amount to more than the saving of refining charges. The fact that the process was tried in Western Australia does not amount to much, for the bullion for the most part produced there is fairly high grade, and efforts have been directed rather to the preliminary treatment in refining than to the melting down of all the dirty accumulations in the zinc boxes, and the subsequent elimination of base metals.

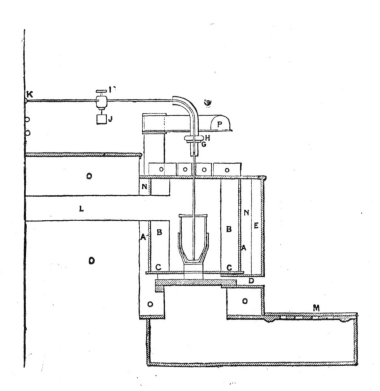

Fig. 1.

CHAPTER VI.

Miller's Process.

The term refining has been very often applied to the removal of base metals from the noble ones, or, in other words, separating the oxidisable from the non-oxidisable ones. When used in this sense it is generally applied to the term bullion, which is an alloy carrying gold and silver, the bullion being pure when it contains gold and silver only. A special term, parting, is borrowed from assaying, and means the separation of gold from silver. In the foregoing processes it is hard to draw the line where one begins and the other ends, but the term refining is used generally here to indicate the separation or partial separation of whatever metals are present with gold.

In order to purify gold and remove the silver from it by any process analogous to the cementation with nitre or salt in a reasonable time, the alloy must be in such a fine state of division that the silver will be removed almost instantly, or diffusion must be assisted by actually keeping the alloy in a molten state. Nitric acid, the active ingredient in the first cementation process described, would not be effective in this case, since even if nitrate of silver did form, the temperature is so high that 'it would be decomposed into oxide of silver, and finally metallic silver and oxides of nitrogen. In fact, nitric acid itself would not be stable at this temperature.

The second active agent was chlorine, or hydrochloric acid, and as the former is known to be much more active than the latter, a process of refining by this means was devised by Mr. Lewis Thompson in 1838. The alloy was melted in a vessel and a stream of chlorine allowed to pass over it. The silver was rapidly converted into chloride, and the gold was
C

thus rendered pure. Later experimentalists found that there was no volatilisation of gold in this process, and that the addition of a chloride of the alkalies or alkaline earths prevented the volatilisation of the chloride of silver formed. It is somewhat difficult to believe that no gold volatilises during such an operation, for if pure gold is heated in a current of chlorine, yellow feathery scales of the chloride will sublime on the upper part of the tube some distance from the flame. This volatilisation is not appreciable until the silver has been removed.

Nearly 30 years after Thompson's discovery, Francis Bowyer Miller, an assayer in the Sydney Mint, discovered and perfected what is known now as Miller's process. He found that by passing chlorine gas into the molten alloy that practically the whole of the chlorine first passed in united with the silver, which in this way could be almost perfectly removed from the bullion as chloride. By passing chlorine over molten alloy the silver would be slowly removed, but most of the chlorine would escape unaltered; the chloride of silver coat also would prevent contact after a short time.

It was assumed by Miller that chloride of gold would not form at the temperature of molten gold, since the compound is decomposed at a dull red heat, but although this assumption was incorrect, the operation of passing chlorine through the molten gold does not allow of volatilisation of the gold while silver is present. The covering of borax and chloride of silver also appears to minimise, if not prevent, this loss.

The process was so successful that it has been adopted at all Australian Mints. Before Miller's invention, the gold coins made at the Sydney Mint were alloyed with silver, since the cost of removing this and replacing it by copper was more than the value of the contained silver.

The following particulars of the operation at the Melbourne branch of the Royal Mint are partly taken from an account supplied to T. Kirk Rose* by Mr. Francis R. Power, and partly from inspection of the process, and particulars kindly supplied through Mr. Wardell, the Deputy Master.

*Metallurgy of Gold, p. 421.

Bullion is received at the Royal Mint in many forms. It comes as alluvial gold, admixed with impurities, as retorted gold, and as smelted gold, more or less admixed with other metals. All classes of bullion are melted with the object of obtaining a sample, the assay of which will accurately represent the bar. Ordinary samples are melted with a flux consisting of

> 100 parts fused borax
> 50 soda carbonate
> 10 nitre.

If the gold is very impure more nitre is added to this flux, a sample is taken to check the subsequent toughening, which is done either with chlorine or nitre until sufficient of the base metals is extracted to enable samples representative of the mass to be taken. Since after weighing and assaying any particular bar loses its individuality, all that is aimed at in the preliminary partial refining is to eliminate any metals or elements which prevent the bullion from being homogeneous, no gold and no silver is removed by this operation.

Furnaces.—The furnaces used for melting the gold are shown in section in Fig. 1. They are cylindrical instead of the usual square sectioned ones, since this form is more economical in fuel, and are more readily cleaned from adhering clinker. They are 12 inches in diameter, and 21 inches deep. Five fire bars, $1\frac{1}{2}$ inches square, and 18 inches long, rest in a cast-iron frame, D, 12 inches by 2 inches, and are supported by a bar at the back. These bars are six inches above the floor. The ash pit, F, is a cast-iron box, below the level of the floor, and the draught passes through a grating at floor level covered with an adjustable damper plate, M. The escaping gases pass through the flue L, which leads to a series of condensing chambers, thence to the stack, which is 80 feet high. The furnace itself is built of arched fire bricks, B, 9 inches by $4\frac{1}{2}$ inches, tapering from $2\frac{3}{4}$ to 2 inches. These are set in an iron cylinder, A, $21\frac{1}{2}$ inches in diameter, and $\frac{3}{8}$ inch thick. The cylinder rests on an iron plate, C, $\frac{5}{8}$ inch thick, and 22 inches in diameter, with a 12 inch hole in the centre. This plate is supported on brickwork. The vertical cylinder is surrounded concrete rammed in, N. When this is set the facing plate is moved out 2 or 3 inches, thus providing an air jacket between the concrete and the external plate of the furnace, keeping the latter cooler. The upper surface of the furnace is also protected by a cast-iron plate. The furnace cover consists of three fireclay tiles, two being 20 inches by 6 inches, the third being smaller—all are bound with iron bands. The middle one is perforated with a $1\frac{1}{2}$ inch hole, through which the chlorine delivery pipe passes.

The Crucibles and Connections.—The pot in which the gold is melted prior to passing chlorine through is made of clay of fine texture, similar to French clay. These are $10\frac{1}{2}$ inches high, 5 inches in diameter, $\frac{3}{8}$ of an inch thick at the top, and gradually increasing to 1 inch at the bottom. These pots are fitted loosely into a guard pot for safety; the guard pot is a plumbago crucible, $8\frac{1}{4}$ inches high, 6 inches internal diameter, $\frac{5}{8}$ inch thick at the top, and $\frac{3}{4}$ of an inch thick at the bottom. This stands in a cylindrical fire brick 5 inches in diameter, and $2\frac{1}{2}$ inches high. Fireclay lids, dished to catch any gold projected by too rapid a current of gas, and having a slit in them to allow of sliding them over the pot without shifting the chlorine pipe are provided.

The pipe stem is 24 inches long, tapering from $\frac{3}{8}$ to $\frac{1}{2}$ an inch at the end inserted into the gold, and is wedge-shaped to facilitate the escape of the chlorine when resting on the bottom of the pot. The bore is $\frac{1}{8}$ inch in diameter. The thin edge of the pipe stem is attached to the branch delivery pipe by a piece of $\frac{1}{2}$ inch rubber, about $2\frac{1}{2}$ inches long, which connects with an ebonite junction, G, 3 inches in length, with a bore of 1-10 inch, turned with a ring round the middle, which acts as a rest for the 8oz. weight, H, used as a sinker for the pipe stem. One end of the ebonite junction is $\frac{1}{2}$ inch in diameter, the other $\frac{3}{4}$ inch, the latter being connected by a stout rubber tube 3 or 4 inches long, to a 14 inch lead pipe, $\frac{1}{2}$ an inch in diameter, which is connected by a rubber junction to a glass stopcock, I, from the spigot of which a $\frac{3}{4}$lb. lead weight, J, is suspended to prevent the pressure of gas from blowing it out.

The Chlorine Generators.—The jar generators described

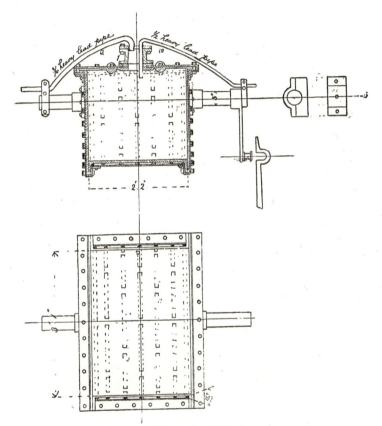

Section Edwards Chlorine Generator.

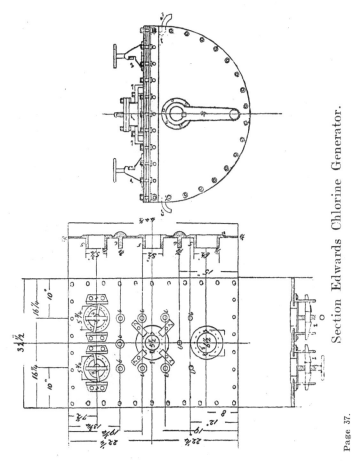

Section Edwards Chlorine Generator.

by Dr. Rose have been thrown out, and two Edwards' Patent Chlorine Generators installed.

These consist of semi-cylindrical vessels hung on trunnions.

The vessel is made of boiler plates riveted together, and lined with sheet lead. The lead is corrugated below so as to give greater strength, but is smooth inside, steam is admitted through a pressure regulator through a trunnion on one side, and fills the space between the lead and iron, thereby providing a steam jacket, the pressure, and therefore the temperature of which is controlled by the regulator; any condensed steam is drained off by means of a pet cock provided; steam escapes through a pipe leading through the other trunnion.

One corner of the generator is attached by means of a connecting rod to a crank which gives it an oscillating motion, thereby preventing the chemicals from packing or becoming baked on the hot lead surface. Holes about 6 inches in diameter left in the flat cover of the generator. These serve for the introduction of the manganese dioxide and acid, and also for washing out the salts. After the charge is exhausted, lead-faced, flat iron covers are removed: these are readily fastened in position by the pressure of a screw bolt at their centre. The screw passes through a horizontal bar, the ends of which slip under projecting lugs riveted on to the generator. The acid is supplied through a siphon pipe near the centre of the flat surface of the generator; the longer limb being sufficient to prevent the acid being thrown out by the internal pressure of the gas.

The chlorine escape pipe passes through the cover, and is connected with a fixed leaden pipe at a point opposite one of the trunnions, so that the oscillation of the generator will only give a minimum movement at this point.

The charge used consists of 100lb. manganese dioxide
        130lb. salt
        275lb. sulphuric acid.

The two generators are used alternately, except when it is required to refine a large amount of gold; in such a case the two generators are used together. When the charge is exhausted in one generator it is connected to the second, and the chlorine gas still remaining is displaced by gradually filling the vessel with water. One of the cover plates is then removed, and the charge is emptied into an underground drain.

The gas passes through a pair of earthenware jars provided with two necks, in which many of the acids or salts mechanically carried over are retained. From these the gas delivery pipe leads to a distributing vessel with two necks, and partly filled with manganese chloride solution. A pressure gauge of 1 inch glass tube 15 feet high is luted to the bottom of this vessel, and fixed to the wall by brackets. Since one inch of gold will balance a column of about 19 inches of water, the liquid in this tube must be from 10 to 11 feet in height to force chlorine through the 7 inches of gold in the pots. The pressure exerted is about 5lb. per square inch. A four-way tube of lead or pottery is pressed through the second neck of the vessel, and each arm is connected by thick rubber to glass stopcocks to which ½ inch lead pipes are joined, these pipes leading to sets of four and five furnaces.

When the flow of chlorine through the gold is stopped the chlorine escapes through a safety pipe. This is provided by having a two-necked earthenware vessel containing such a quantity of water that when the pressure of the gas exceeds the working pressure required, the end of a glass tube, passing to the bottom of the vessel, and connected above the neck with a 4 inch lead pipe ten feet high, becomes unsealed, and the gas escapes through the water in large bubbles, passing thence through a glass pipe inclined at an angle at the top of the lead pipe into the air. When sufficient gas has escaped to reduce the pressure to the working limit the pipe is automatically sealed.

All rubber junctions are covered with calico, and painted, and where practicable secured with copper wire.

Passing the Gas Through the Molten Metal.—The guard with the clay liner is placed in the furnace, and 2 or 3 ounces of fused borax added. It is heated until dull red. The ingots are then added, the weight of these being about 700oz. Fuel is added, and the dampers opened. As soon as the gold is

Another View of Edwards' Generator.

melted, the lid is put on and the pipe stem, carefully annealed and heated to bright redness, is pushed to the bottom of the pot, chlorine at the same time being gently turned on to avoid the plugging of the tube through the gold solidifying in it. The supply of chlorine is adjusted so as to avoid projection of globules. This can be told by feeling the pulsations of the rubber—when the gold contains much silver or base metals the absorption of the chlorine takes place rapidly but quietly, very little motion of the molten metal being apparent, but near the end of the operation the gas must be admitted in a fine stream only. The chlorine is not dried before it passes into the gold, but the small amount of water vapor present does not affect the operation. It was formerly the practice to dry the gas with strong sulphuric acid, but this has been abandoned as unnecessary.

The order in which the metals chloridise has never been determined. Iron appears to come off separately, and is attacked at the commencement, while silver and copper remain and come off practically together.

When the bullion contains much base metal the consumption of chlorine is greater, and the time occupied longer, but not in proportion to the amount contained, since a more rapid stream of chlorine can be safely admitted than when the base metals and silver are nearly all removed.

The usual time allowed is four hours for a pot containing about 700oz. of bullion. If the bullion is nearly fine a much shorter time would suffice; for instance, 2 per cent. of silver and 0.5 per cent. of base would take about $1\frac{1}{2}$ hours; 3.5 of silver and 1.5 of base, two hours.

Owing to the presence of air at first in the chlorine mains the stream admitted is slow at first, otherwise there is danger of spitting.

When the operation is nearing completion the flame issuing from the holes or slit in the lid becomes small, and alters in appearance; it becomes very luminous, has a brown edge, and if a white, rough, cold surface is plunged into it will become coated with a yellowish-brown tinge. It consists mainly of ferric chloride, with traces of silver chloride and gold. As soon as this stain appears the current of gas is reduced, and

allowed to pass in for another 15 minutes, when the clay pipe
is withdrawn, and the clay pot lifted out of the guard pot. The
pot is allowed to stand under a hood to carry off the fumes
until the gold has solidified.   The liquid chloride and fluxes
are then poured into a mould provided with a hood. The pot
is then broken, and the cone of gold dropped into the guard
pot, and cast into two flat ingots, 12 by 4 by 1½ inches. These
bars, while still hot, are dropped in dilute sulphuric acid, and
then water, and are still hot enough to become dry.

A modification of the process has been introduced. After
the chlorine has been passed into the bullion for some time the
chloride of silver which forms occupies twice the space that
the silver did, and rises in the pot.   When much silver was
present the chloride was ladled out from time to time, to
prevent it overflowing, and poured into a mould on top of the
furnace.   This practice has now been adopted for all the
bullion. The chloride is baled out in such a way that any drip
falls back again into the crucible.   When the chloride film
becomes thin some gold is also picked up—the last pourings
are, therefore, put into a separate mould, when the gold present solidifies, the chloride is poured off, and the gold returned
to the crucible. The last portion of silver remains on top of
the gold, bone ash is added to thicken it, after which the refined gold is stirred and poured, the pot being returned at once
to the furnace to be used for a fresh lot of bullion.

The chlorides contain 5 to 10 per cent. of gold in feathery
particles. Generally speaking the gold is not present as
chloride when the chlorine is passing, but chloride of gold has
been found in the silver chloride when the process has been
experimentally carried too far. The chlorides are supersaturated
with chlorine and this is copiously evolved on cooling. To recover this gold 7 per cent. of their weight of bicarbonate of soda
is added cautiously and without stirring, which produces a
shower of globules of reduced silver, and these, falling
through the chlorides, carry down nearly all the gold; another
lot is needed to carry the balance down. The pot is lifted out,
the button allowed to settle and solidify, when the chlorides
are poured into a mould 12 by 10 by 2 inches. The silvery button obtained contains from 40 to 60 per cent. of gold. The

Ingots of Base Metal.

gold in bars and in the buttons contain 99.85 per cent. of the gold issued for refining, the balance being practically in the pot. The maximum quantity left in the silver is 1 part in 10,000, but it is usually from half to one-third of this quantity.

The cakes of impure chloride of silver are sewn up in coarse flannel bags and boiled with water in a wooden vat for four or five hours. The salt present in the cake helps in the solution of the cuprous chloride present. The cakes are placed ultimately with wrought plates $\frac{1}{8}$ inch thick, in a cast iron tank lined with similar plates. The plates are prevented from touching the bags by means of laths of wood, otherwise copper would be reduced in the bags and would be difficult to separate from the silver. The reduction is slow on starting, unless either some liquid is left from some previous operation or some chloride of iron is added. The bath must be heated by a jet of steam and kept boiling from two to four days. When the operation is complete no hard lumps can be felt in the bag. The silver is reduced in this way while the copper is not. When reduction is complete the silver is washed and smelted without fluxes, the average grade of the metal so produced being about 980. The total loss of silver amounts to about 1.6 per cent.

CHAPTER VII.

Parting by Means of Nitric Acid. — This process
is of great antiquity, and probably dates from the
discovery of nitric acid; it is one of the simplest parting processes, and does not require a costly plant or much manipula-
tive skill.   The main objection to it is the cost of the acid.
The operation comprises the preparation of a suitable alloy.
It was formerly considered that three parts of silver to one of
gold was necessary, hence the term inquartation process; it
has been found, however, that a very much lesser quantity
suffices if more than one treatment with acid is given.   Kerl
states that if all the silver is to be dissolved from gold by one
boiling with nitric acid the amount of silver must be at least
eight times the weight of the gold.   When the proportion,
$1:2\frac{1}{2}$, is parted, the resulting gold is left as a porous sponge, if
dilute acid is used for the first treatment.   Silver is not
essential as an alloying metal, for other metals soluble in
nitric acid may be used.   However, if silver contains even a
small amount of gold it would be better to use the metal
rather than an equivalent amount of any other. When another
metal is used, the weight need not necessarily be so great as
that of silver.   Parting appears to depend upon the space
occupied by the molecules of the alloying metal, also upon
the molecules of the acid and of the products which form and
their relative dilution; the temperature and time of action are
also essential factors.   Dealing with the first point, if
approximately two of silver are used to one of gold we would
have an alloy whose approximate formula is $Au\,Ag_4$. When

the silver is dissolved from this alloy the mass holds together. The particles of gold are therefore close enough to cohere. Since the atomic volume of gold and that of silver are approximately equal, by choosing some other metal whose molecules occupy the same space as the silver, it should be possible to remove this in the same way. Taking zinc for example. If the gold zinc alloy be made according to the formula Au. $Zn._4$, the amount of zinc to be added need only be 1.3 to 1 of gold.

If sodium were used the alloy Au. Na_4 would have only one-half the sodium as the gold. In this case also the high atomic volume of the sodium would serve to separate the molecules of gold further from each other. Admixtures of metals such as silver and copper also serve the same end as silver by passing into solution, allowing the acid to pass between the particles of gold.

An amalgam of mercury, silver, and gold can also be parted by means of nitric acid, but if the gold-silver alloy is rich in gold the separation of silver is incomplete. When gold is parted from such an amalgam it will be found to be in fine crystals.

Since no authentic information as to the ratio of other metals required for parting is to be found in current literature, a number of experiments were made to determine whether lesser quantities of metals might be used. The old term inquartation assumed a ratio of 3 of silver to 1 of gold, and this ratio is quoted even now as being necessary for parting operations. It is well known to assayers that $2\frac{1}{2}$ or $2\frac{1}{4}$ of silver to one of gold will part as well as 3 to 1, but how much less is sufficient was determined experimentally.

The acid used was nitric, 68 per cent. strength, and two strengths were used, the dilute being made by mixing two volumes of water with one volume of acid, the second by taking one of each; the term strong acid means the 68 per cent. acid. The gold taken in the three cases was 10 grains, the silver 10, 15, 20 grains, or in ratios of 1 to 1, 1.5 to 1, 2 to 1. The alloy was made by wrapping the metals in lead and cupelling; the buttons were afterwards flattened and rolled into strips of uniform thickness.

No. of sample	Ratio of silver to gold	Action of dilute acid after boiling for 30 minutes and color of cornet	Action of 1 of nitric to 1 of water	Weight of cornet
A	1:1	No brown fumes. Light brown color, silvery in patches	No fumes	Not weighed
B	1.5:1	No brown fumes. Dull yellow-ish brown, silvery in patches.	Brown fumes color of cornet not altered	Not weighed
C	2:1	Brown fumes. Dull brown	Brown fumes	10.004

A, B, and C were then boiled with 5cc. of strong acid, washed, dried, and weighed. The weights were—

A—13.157.
B—10.050.
C— 9.990.

It is therefore clear that 2 of silver and 1 of gold are sufficient for parting, and that 1.5 to one is ample if the resultant gold is subsequently treated by sulphuric acid or bisulphate of sodium. The action on 1 of silver to one of gold was not complete in the time allowed, the weaker acids had practically no effect, and there is little doubt had the strong acid been allowed to act for a longer time that much more silver would have been removed.

Parting of Zinc and Gold. — In order to find what proportion of zinc would be required, 10 grains of gold and 10 grains of zinc were melted together in a porcelain crucible, using potassium cyanide as a cover to exclude air. The alloy melted quietly at a comparatively low temperature. The KCy was washed out and the solid button was treated with 40cc. of 1 to 1 nitric acid. The zinc was violently attacked, and the button became fissured through the rapid evolution of gas. After boiling for half an hour the solution was poured off and the bead washed with water; 20cc. of strong nitric was then added, and the solution boiled for five minutes.

The button was washed and weighed. The weight was 10.586. It is probable had the action of the acid been continued for a few minutes longer that the zinc would have been removed.

The button was next fused with $NaHSO_4$, washed, heated, and the weight was 10.054 grains. This on cupellation gave a button weighing 9947 grains. It would appear therefore that some gold dissolves in the strong nitric acid, even though some zinc is still left in the button.

Parting of Zinc, Silver, and Gold.—Since the removal, not of zinc, but of silver is aimed at in parting, an alloy consisting of—

> Gold, 9.000,
> Silver, 1.000,
> Zinc, 10.000,

was fused in a porcelain crucible under a layer of potassium cyanide. After cleaning the button, it was boiled for half an hour with 20cc of 2 of nitric acid to 1 of water. The zinc dissolved first, and white silver-like crystals appeared on washing with water after first treatment by acid. The button became fissured. The acid was poured off, and 10cc of 1 to 1 acid put on and boiled for about 15 minutes; finally 5cc of strong nitric were applied. The button was washed, dried and weighed. The weight of gold was 9023. It was then wrapped in sheet lead and cupelled. The final weight was 8885. In this case, as in the previous one, some solution of the gold takes place, even although the whole of the zinc was not removed.

The ratio of the gold-zinc alloy would give a formula approaching Au. Zn_8, which seems to be sufficient for parting. It therefore follows that zinc could be substituted for silver in this operation. It has the advantage of being cheap, of forming an alloy at a low temperature, and even when in small proportions it reacts vigorously with nitric acid.

Parting of Copper and Gold. — If parting depended on the formula alone, assuming that the alloying metal was dissolved by nitric acid, then copper should do as well as zinc, since the atomic weights are nearly equal. In order to determine this an alloy of 10.008 of gold and 10.080 of copper was made and placed in 1 of nitric to 2 of water and boiled. The solution was almost unaffected, showing that this alloy is not attacked by very dilute acid; the alloy was then immersed in a solution of 1 of nitric to 1 of water and boiled; the solution became light green colour, showing that the attack of the acid had commenced; the action, however, was so slight that the strong acid was used. This solution was colored green almost immediately, and brown fumes were evolved. Boiling was continued for some hours, and the fresh acid added from time to time as long as it became green. When the solution did not react for copper the button was washed, dried and heated. It weighed 9789. On cupellation this went 9746, showing that gold dissolved in the nitric acid. even though copper remained in the bead. Thus, althcugh the action took place with copper as with zinc, it was much slower, and stronger acid had to be used to start the attack.

Sodium and Gold. — In order to find out the effect of metallic sodium on gold in parting, an alloy of gold, silver and sodium was made by melting—

    4.4grms. gold, or 62 per cent. Au.

    1.7grms. silver, or 24 per cent. Ag.

    1grm. sodium, or 14 per cent. Na.. in a hard
        glass tube.

The mixture melted at a dull red heat.

On removing the same, and placing in water, a copious evolution of hydrogen took place, and the alloy, instead of being silvery white, like amalgam, became light bronze yellow, and appeared to be made of a mass of coherent crystals, which would crumble to powder under pressure. An assay of this product, after water treatment, gave

    Gold,   64.7

    Silver,   23.4

    Scdium,   11.9

A portion of the alloy was boiled with dilute, then strong nitric acid, but it did not wholly part, the gold button remaining being only 964 fine.

By taking a somewhat greater proportion of sodium, parting can be effected by means of nitric acid. This alloy, as will be shown, will part with sulphuric acid, followed by fusion with nitre cake.

Tellurium in Gold. — Some time ago the author

was struck with the fact that a comparatively low amount of tellurium in gold bullion enabled nitric acid to dissolve out a large proportion of the silver, even when the latter was present in a lesser extent than half the gold. The general explanation must be in this case, as well as in that of sodium, that small proportions of these elements occupy comparatively large spaces between the individual particles of gold, thus enabling the solvents to penetrate. The temperature of the acid, and its strength, and the time of application are also governing factors.

CHAPTER VIII.

Parting with Nitric Acid on a Large Scale.

The method of parting with nitric acid usually consists in

(1) Granulating the alloy, which should be free from antimony, tin, or sulphides.

(2) Treating with dilute nitric acid, and decanting the solution.

(3) Boiling with strong nitric acid.

(4) Washing the parted gold free from alloy.

(5) Smelting the parted gold.

(6) Recovering the silver from solution.

The granulating is done by melting the alloy and pouring it into cold water, in such a way that the granules do not stick under the water. This operation can be carried on by allowing the stream of molten metal strike the edge of an inclined plate before falling into water. In this way more shell-like granules will be formed.   It is inadvisable to have shotty and solid lumps amongst the granules, for the time of solution will be governed by the diameter of these. The water should be kept cool, for the molten metal can sometimes be seen to be red hot below its surface, and if it is all poured in one place an adherent pyramid of the granules may be lifted out. The pots used for parting consist of porcelain, or well glazed earthenware. Those used in the American Mints were about 21 inches in diameter, and 22 inches deep, provided with handles and a spout.   125lb. of granulated bullion is put in each of the pots.   The pots are set in tanks containing water, which is heated by steam coils. Each pot is provided with a wooden lath, which acts as a stirrer.*

The acid used on a large scale appears to have been much too strong. Johnson and Matthey boiled the alloy with three lots of acid, 50 pints, 30 pints, and 20 pints respectively, for 4, 3, and 2 hours, when parting 800oz. of bullion.† The last acid was used over again, as it contained very little silver. The strength of the acid being 1.4 sp. gr., diluted with its own volume of water. The acid used in the San Francisco Mint was ordinary strong acid, 1.4 sp. gr. In neither case was any attempt made to re-convert any of the oxide of nitrogen escaping into fresh acid.

The amount of nitric acid required to dissolve a metal depends on the amount of acid present, and temperature, as well as the nature and weight of metal. If the acid is strong and hot the higher oxides of nitrogen are evolved, but if weak and cold no gas at all may come off; in the latter case nitrous oxide, or even ammonia may form. Even when hot concentrated acid is used the reactions which go on cannot be expressed by one formula, for, on dissolving zinc with such an acid, although nitrogen peroxide is abundantly given off, nitrate of ammonia will be found on evaporating the solution to dryness. Copper and zinc, on account of their lower equivalent weights, will consume more nitric acid than silver; zinc also appears to have a greater reducing power on the acid than either of the others. The most economical strength of acid for any given alloy is readily determined by taking a known weight, and estimating the free acid left over after dissolving as much as will pass into solution in a given time. As a rule the lower the products of oxidation evolved the less will be the acid consumption; for instance, with silver, if nitrogen peroxide, nitric oxide or nitrate of ammonia is found according to the following equations:—

$$Ag + 2HNO_3 = AgNO_3 + NO_2 + H_2O.$$
$$(2)\ 6Ag + 8HNO_3 = 6AgNO_3 + 2NO + 4H_2O.$$
$$(3)\ 8Ag + 10HNO_3 = 8AgNO_3 + NH_4NO_3 + 3H_2O$$

*Eggleston, Metallurgy of Gold, Silver, Mercury, p. 705.
†Percy, Metallurgy of Gold, p. 477.

D

In other words, the amount of acid used up or neutralised would be in the proportion of 1 for the first case, 0.66 for the second, and 0.62 for the third case. After boiling in the first acid, and after the action has ceased, as may be observed by the cessation of the evolution of brown fumes, hot water should be added, to prevent the deposition of silver nitrate crystals, and to give more liquor for the decantation of the silver solution. It is preferable to remove as much of the silver nitrate in solutions as possible by decanting it by means of a siphon, and replacing with water free from chlorine and again decanting, before adding the second lot of acid. Very little silver is removed by the second acid, and this solution, as well as a third, may be again used on a fresh lot of bullion. After the acid treatment, the gold is washed with hot water and well stirred, allowed to settle, and the supernatant liquid removed. When the reaction for silver is slight, the metal is removed and washed on a filter until the silver nitrate is removed—sometimes a wash with ammonia water is given in order to remove any chloride which may have remained. The gold precipitate is then pressed, dried, and heated to redness, and smelted, the bars usually running 995 to 998 fine.

Parting Zinc Cyanide Bullion. — A modification of the process is sometimes made use of in treatment of the bullion obtained from the precipitation of gold and silver on zinc filaments in the cyanide process. The operations are as follow :—

(1) The removal of the bullion from the zinc filaments.

(2) Smelting the same, so as to obtain a low-grade bullion.

(3) Granulation of the alloy so obtained.

(4) Parting with nitric acid.

(5) Recovering silver from the solutions.

The zinc filaments, as well as any finely divided precipitated metals, are removed from the zinc boxes, and passed through a sieve having about 50 to 60 holes per linear inch. The finely divided precipitated metals pass through—the coarser zinc fragments are retained and replaced in the box for further use; the fine material is allowed to settle, the water is decanted, and the slimes are

washed by filtration or in a filter press. They are then removed
and gently dried in a cast-iron tube set in brickwork, and
heated externally. The cylinder is open one end, and having
an exhaust pipe at the other leading to a pipe which acts as
an atmospheric condenser—mercury is often caught in this.
The slimes are thus dried and partly oxidised. They are then
mixed with suitable fluxes so as to slag off the oxides present,
and collect the bullion on melting. During the fusion some of
the zinc is volatilised, but part of it alloys with the
other metals, and melts down. So long as about 45 per cent.
is present the alloy will part with nitric acid when granulated.

The composition of such an alloy may be indicated by
the following proximate analysis:—

Gold   40—45 per cent.
Silver   15—20 per cent.
Lead   2—4   per cent.
Copper   1—2   per cent.
Zinc   40—30 per cent.

This alloy is granulated, then parted first with dilute
nitric acid, the nitrates formed are partly removed by washing
with water; strong nitric acid is then added, and the granules
boiled for some time. The liquid is decanted, the granules
washed and smelted. The silver is precipitated as chloride
with salt, washed, treated with zinc, and the reduced silver
washed, dried and smelted.

Double Acid Parting. — A double system for parting was introduced in the San Francisco and Philadelphia
Mints. Nitric acid, as previously described, was used for the
preliminary removal of silver: 135lb. of the granulations were
heated with 125lb. of strong nitric acid; the alloy stirred with
a wooden lath every twenty minutes. The water bath sur-
rounding the pots was kept boiling for twelve hours; water was
added, and the nitrate of silver decanted. An additional quantity of acid was added, and after twelve hours' boiling this was
removed and applied to a fresh lot of bullion, since it contained
very little silver. The gold remaining was washed first by decantation in the pot, and was then removed and washed in a
shallow vat provided with a false bottom, covered with a filter.
Hot water was allowed to run through until all the soluble ni-

trate of silver had been removed.   The gold now containing
only a small proportion of silver was ladled into cast-iron pots
provided with a hood to carry away fumes, sulphuric acid sufficient to cover the gold was added, and the mass evaporated
almost to dryness; a small amount of nitre was added to make
the gold denser; more sulphuric acid. 92 per cent. in strength,
was added and heated, and the gold stirred with an iron rod.
The acid was poured or ladled out, the gold removed, washed
on a filter with hot water, dried and smelted into bars which
assayed 998 fine.

CHAPTER IX.

The Recovery of Silver from Nitrate Solutions. — The usual method of recovering silver from these solutions is to precipitate the silver by means of common salt. From an ordinary alloy the only salts likely to be precipitated are mercurous chloride and lead chloride. The former would be present in traces only, and would be eliminated in subsequent operations. Lead is generally removed before smelting, but assuming any to be present it will be thrown down. The salt should be added from a saturated solution, and should only be in slight excess.

$$Ag\ NO_3 + NaCl = AgCl + NaNO_3$$

Copper, zinc, and other soluble nitrates and chlorides remain in solution.

The solution should be well mixed and stirred together, for the clots of silver chloride retain some nitrate. The precipitate should then be allowed to settle, and the clear solution decanted off, and, if necessary, run through a filter. The silver chloride is then washed with water until the washings are neutral. It is then reduced by zinc or iron.

On a large scale a lead-lined box or vat serves for the reduction. The silver chloride is introduced, then the zinc required for the reduction added.

$$Zn + 2AgCl = Zn\ Cl_2 + 2Ag.$$

At least 65 parts by weight of zinc to 287 of silver chloride. The zinc is added in the form of granules, and these must be well mixed with the chloride. If the action of reduction does not start at once, a small amount of sulphuric must be added. If the chloride is dry a small amount of water must be added to keep the zinc chloride and sulphate in solution. The reduction is complete in about four hours. When the silver is all in the metallic state, as may be tested by withdrawing some of the sludge, washing it with water, and then finding whether it is wholly soluble in nitric acid, enough sulphuric acid is added to dissolve any excess of zinc added. After the action is complete the excess of liquor is decanted; fresh water is run on, the precipitate is allowed to settle, and again decanted. It can be finally washed by being placed on filter cloth laid over the perforated lead bottom of a small vat. Hot water is run on until the washings are wholly free from sulphuric acid. The precipitated silver is then pressed into blocks, and dried in a furnace, after which it is smelted into bars. As a rule it is very nearly pure; any lead present may be removed by adding some silver sulphate crystals when melting.

CHAPTER X.

Refining by Means of Sulphuric Acid.

Pure silver is readily attacked by strong hot sulphuric acid of sp. gr. 1.815, or about 90 per cent. strength. The reaction which takes place may be represented as follows:—

$$2Ag + 2H_2SO_4 = Ag_2SO_4 + 2H_2O + SO_2.$$

Silver sulphate so produced is very soluble in the strong acid, when it is hot, as little as one-fourth of its weight of sulphuric acid being sufficient. As a matter of fact, on applying the acid the bisulphate of silver forms which melts at a comparatively low temperature.

$$2Ag + 3H_2SO_4 = 2Ag HSO_4 + 2H_2O + SO_2$$

When the melted mass is cooled the bisulphate crystallises out. By pouring the solution out into water a copious white precipitate of the bisulphate forms. If, however, the solution is carefully diluted by means of steam to about a sp. gr. of 1.65 or 73 per cent. sulphuric acid, and allowed to cool, hard yellow crystals of anhydrous silver sulphate are precipitated. The same crystals may be obtained by allowing an aqueous solution, or one of dilute sulphuric acid, containing the bisulphate in solution to cool down; a deposit of yellow crystals of Ag_2SO_4 will form.

Dr. Percy[*] states that one part of silver sulphate requires for its solution

180 parts of cold water

88 parts of boiling water.

180 parts of cold sulphuric acid, 10deg. B. (or sp. gr. 1.07, about 9 per cent.)

[*] Gold and Silver, p. 459.

30 parts of boiling sulphuric acid 10deg. B. (or sp. gr. 1.07, about 9 per cent.)

20 parts of boiling sulphuric acid, 20deg. B. (or sp. gr. 1.16, about 18 per cent.)

4 parts of cold sulphuric acid, 66B. (or sp. gr. 1.81, about 90 per cent.)

¼ part of boiling sulphuric acid, 66 (or sp. gr. 1.81, about 90 per cent.)

55 parts of boiling solution of sulphate of copper, 10deg. B.

45 parts of boiling solution of sulphate of copper, 20 deg. B.

35 parts of boiling acid of sulphate of copper, 10deg. B.

Additional figures will be submitted subsequently.

No information could be gained as to the relative amounts of metals necessary for parting with sulphuric acid. It is obvious that for successful parting the metal dissolved must form a compound easily soluble in the solvent, otherwise the insoluble sulphate or compound formed will coat the alloy, and prevent further action. Copper, iron and zinc form such insoluble salts, silver sulphate is readily soluble in strong sulphuric acid, and also sodium sulphate.

Parting Gold-silver Alloy with Sulphuric Acid.—Alloys of 10 grains of gold, assaying 9992, were taken, and alloyed with 10, 15, 20 grains of fine silver respectively. Each alloy was rolled out in the same manner as was adoped for the nitric acid parting; 20cc of strong sulphuric, 92 per cent., acid was used in each case, and the cornets were boiled for one hour. The resulting gold was much paler in colour than when nitric acid was used on similar alloys. The alloy containing equal quantities of gold and silver appeared to be such a pale yellow colour that it was not anticipated that anything more than a superficial action had gone on. The acid was poured off, and the cornets washed with distilled water, then dried and weighed. The results are as follow:—

Number	Composition silver	gold	Weight of gold	Weight after fusion with NaHSO$_4$
A	10	10	10.064	9975
B	15	10	9.998	—
C	20	10	9.992	—

It is, therefore, clear that strong sulphuric will separate practically all the gold from an alloy of one of gold to one of silver, and that its action is much more complete than nitric acid on such an alloy.

To determine how zinc, silver, gold alloy would part, those metals were melted together in the following proportions:—

Gold   9975
Silver   983
Zinc 10,100

Owing to the energy with which zinc and gold combine a small portion was lost through spitting.

The alloy was washed with water, then heated with dilute sulphuric acid (1 in 10), hydrogen was evolved freely. Ten cc. of strong sulphuric were added, and the solution boiled for one hour. The acid was poured off, and distilled water placed on the brown button left. It immediately became white, owing to the precipitation of the silver in solution on the zinc.

$$Ag_2 SO_4 + Zn = 2Ag + Zn SO_4.$$

On adding more acid, and boiling, and then washing with water and dilute nitric acid the weight of the bead was 9750. On cupelling it weighed 9658. The button still contained silver. It is, therefore, not practicable to part such zinc, silver, gold, alloys with sulphuric acid, even although such alloys will part readily with nitric acid.

Gold, Silver, and Sodium.—An alloy was then taken consisting of:—

Gold   64.7
Silver   23.4
Sodium   11.9

This was boiled in dilute, then in strong sulphuric acid, gave gold 988 fine; this when fused with sodium bisulphate gave gold 993 fine. This shows that a very small amount of sodium is sufficient for parting with sulphuric acid. The alloy requires such a low temperature for melting, and parting can be done so easily, and there is no impurity introduced which cannot easily be eliminated.   With sodium at a low price the method of parting could be advantageously practised in many cases.

Effect of Tellurium on Parting. — This experiment was made to see if comparatively small quantities of tellurium had the same effect as sodium in enabling acid solutions to dissolve out silver from gold bullion. An alloy of gold and silver, containing 72.14 per cent. of gold, the balance being almost pure silver, was taken and melted with tellurium in a reducing flame.

Alloy	17.321
Tellurium	2.143
Total	19.464

After being gently warmed with sulphuric the characteristic crimson colour denoting the solution of tellurium appeared; the alloy was boiled for one hour with strong sulphuric acid; it was then washed and dried. It weighed 19.114. The acid had, therefore, only dissolved a small portion of the silver and tellurium.

It was then treated with 1cc of sulphuric acid, and 10 grms. sodium bisulphate, and heated to dull redness; a violent action went on, and silver, as well as tellurium dissolved. After washing the soluble salts away the button was cut with a knife. The outside had been attacked, and the solvent had penetrated for about 1-16th of an inch, but the inside was lead grey and waxy. The button was broken into three pieces (a small amount was lost in so doing), and sulphuric acid again added, with a few crystals of sodium nitrate. A strong purple colour showed that tellurium was dissolving, five grammes of sodium bisulphate were subsequently added, and heat applied to redness. The slag was yellow hot and faintly greenish in cooling. On washing with water a voluminous precipitate of tellurous acid separated out. This was readily soluble in dilute sulphuric acid.   The gold remaining was dried, and weighed 12.245grs. It was then parted in the usual way, and the parted gold weighed 12.005 grains. The fineness of the gold was, therefore, 98.04. This experiment shows that gold only 64.2 fine can be raised to nearly pure gold through the presence of about 10 per cent. of tellurium. If the alloy had been crushed to a fine powder, or even granulated, the action would have been more rapid. Solid masses containing only a relatively small amount of soluble material are difficult to decompose with solvent. The solvent has to find its way through the insoluble material, and if the spaces between the particles are small, the friction is very great; secondly the substance dissolved must diffuse in an opposite direction into the body of the solvent, and thirdly, the evolution of gas, which generally takes place from the particles attacked, has to escape, and thereby checks the inward flow of the solvent. The retardation of solvent action must, therefore, increase with the thickness of alloy to be penetrated.

Parting of Gold and Silver Commercially. — Gold is not soluble in sulphuric acid except when nitric acid or some other oxidising agent is present. In this case it is again precipitated on dilution with water. Neither platinum nor palladium are dissolved when these are present in a silver alloy.

Copper is dissolved when alloyed with silver, but owing to the insolubility of copper sulphate in strong sulphuric acid the action is either retarded or prevented. Copper, also, owing to its low equivalent, consumes nearly three and a half times as much sulphuric acid as silver.

Zinc behaves in a similar manner to copper.

Iron is also slowly attacked, white iron, containing phosphorus, being less attacked than grey pig. The sulphate of iron formed is insoluble in strong sulphuric acid.

Tin and antimony are also dissolved, but form basic salts on dilution.

Lead is slowly attacked, if in large quantities, but in small it dissolves readily. If present in excess lead sulphate separates out from strong acid solution. On dilution with water the lead sulphate dissolved by the strong acid is thrown down.

From the foregoing facts in separating gold from silver

it is advisable to have only the two metals present; small amounts of other metals do not interfere, but large amounts occasion trouble. For this reason base bullion is usually first treated by a process of liquation to eliminate the copper. If the base alloy be placed in a lead bath, heated strongly, the gold and silver will dissolve in the lead, while the copper, on cooling down, will form an alloy with the lead, and float on the top. It may then be stiffened with ashes or such material as will entangle it, and scraped off. The gold and silver can be obtained free from other metals by a process of scorification, or, as is termed on a large scale, cupellation, the oxide of lead serving to oxidise and carry off chemically or mechanically metals such as arsenic, antimony, or tin. The bullion, if in suitable proportions, is then ready for parting.

Outline of the sulphuric acid process as originally used in the New York assay office. The process comprised eight operations :—

(1) Inquarting and granulating the bullion.
(2) Solution of the granulated bullion in sulphuric acid.
(3) Smelting of the fusion of the insoluble residue of gold.
(4) Condensation of the acid fumes.
(5) Reduction of the silver sulphates by copper.
(6) Sweetening and melting the precipitated copper.
(7) Treatment of the sulphate of copper.
(8) Treatment of bye products.

The alloys were made so as to contain from two to four of silver to one of gold. This was then melted. If iridosmine happened to be present, the parcel which contained it was melted with four or five times its weight of silver, mainly to decrease the density of the alloy; the platinum metals sank to the bottom. The molten alloy of silver and gold was then slowly poured out, taking care to leave the heavy metals in the bottom. More silver was added, and the process repeated until at last the amount of gold remaining was trifling. The "King," or separated portion of the silver-gold alloy was then dealt with by itself, and the silver parted from it. The alloy of gold and silver was again melted and poured from a height of a few feet with a wavy motion into a vessel filled with water, which was kept cool.

The granulated bullion was introduced into cast iron pots of the following dimensions:—45in. diameter, 26in. deep, holding about 160 gallons of acid. Each pot is provided with a hemispherical hood, lined with lead, and connected on to the acid condensing chamber. Openings in the hood are provided for stirring the granulations or introducing material.

The charge of alloy was from 300 to 400lbs. and the amount of acid used was usually four times the weight of the alloy. After being boiled several hours, the solution was run off by means of a siphon, care being taken not to remove any gold. This was attained by turning up the end of the siphon for about three inches. Fresh acid is introduced, and the gold is withdrawn by means of a perforated ladle, and placed in a scoop. This gold was then placed in a smaller pot and more acid added and boiled. This operation was repeated five times. The gold was then placed in a tub and washed, first with cold water and then with hot. Very often lead sulphate is left with the gold, but by carefully running a stream of water over the gold, placed on an inclined slab, it may be washed away mechanically. After this it is boiled again with sulphuric acid if necessary, until, on melting, the bullion is brought up to 998 fine. In all about seven boilings with acids were required, the operations taking five days.

The Gutzkow Process.—The next improvement in the parting of gold and silver is due to Gutzkow. This was introduced into the San Francisco Assaying and Refining Works in 1867. Briefly, it consists of parting the alloy with strong sulphuric acid in iron pots, removing the solution containing sulphate of silver, diluting and cooling this to cause a deposition of crystals of the same; the acid thus freed from the sulphate of silver is used over again. The sulphate of silver itself was reduced by running a saturated solution of ferrous sulphate over it.

For this process when the alloy was rich in gold, such, for instance, as from two parts of gold to three parts of silver, it was granulated before parting; when it was poor in gold, such as when it contained from one of gold to five or more of silver, it was introduced into the acid in bricks or bars. Solution took place just as readily in the latter case, because there was less need for regulating the temperature in order to avoid frothing. Full descriptions of this process are to be found in Eggleston. Gold and Mercury, vol. II., p. 775, and in Percy, Silver and Gold, p. 479, and since the process has been improved upon nothing further need be said about it here.

The improvements made by Gutzkow on his process consist mainly in decomposing the crystals of sulphate of silver by heating them in a crucible with carbon. The improved process is in use in several parts of Australia.*

The following description is taken, mainly from a paper by Mr. G. H. Blakemore.† The requirements are:—

1. One '400 gallon tank set on a stand eight feet high. This tank supplies the necessary water; either hot or cold.
2. A cast-iron parting kettle, with movable cast-iron hood. The kettle should hold 1000lbs. of strong sulphuric acid. It is set over a fireplace.
3. A small lead condenser to catch sulphuric acid and other vapors from the kettle. This is 10 feet x 7 feet x 5 feet, and is built with 4lb. to square foot lead.
4. Two cast-iron pans. 6 feet x 3 feet x 1 foot.
5. Two lead lined wooden boxes, with antimonial-lead plug cocks. Boxes are 2 feet x 18 inches x 18 inches.
6. One lead lined wooden box, 6 feet x 1 foot 6 inches x 1 foot 6 inches, to hold precipitated copper.
7. One recovery box, eight compartments, made of 2in. soft pine, each compartment 2 feet wide, 4 feet deep, 4 feet long. This is filled with scrap iron.
8. Fire drying pan of castiron, 5 feet x 2 feet 6 inches x 6 inches deep, set over fireplace.
9. Three leaden buckets to hold acids.
10. One iron paddle, 4 feet long, of $\frac{3}{4}$ inch round iron.
11. One iron ladle, to hold about one pint, $\frac{3}{4}$ inch iron handle.
12. Two trowel-shaped tools.

---

*Eggleston, Gold and Silver, p. 750.
†Transactions of the Australian Institute of Mining Engineers, vol. V., p. 253.

13. Six wooden paddles, one inch round handle, blade of paddle, 6 inches x 4 inches.

14. Set of hydrometers.

18. Melting furnace for gold.

19. Rubber gum boots and gloves.

20. Steam pipes with rubber connections and lead pipes.

21. Water pipes to various places, also rubber hose and roses.

A charge for such a plant is 200lbs. dore bullion or thereabouts. From 1¼ to 1½lbs. of concentrated acid per lb. of bullion is placed on the dore bars. The acid is boiled for about two hours. Two jars of the acid obtained at a subsequent stage are added and boiling continued for from three to four hours, when all the silver will be found in solution. The kettle is then filled up to within about an inch from the top with the acid before mentioned, so that about four pounds of acid are present for every pound of dore charged. When the cold acid is added there is a copious precipitate of bisulphate and sulphate of silver. In order to get this into solution it is sometimes necessary to re-heat the solution. When the silver has dissolved, the ladle is used, and the gold, which settles in a pocket cast in the bottom of the kettle, removed. When the gold powder is removed, the kettle is allowed to stand half an hour, and the contents are siphoned out by means of a piece of bent gas tube pipe, to within two inches of the bottom, into a cast-iron pan. Steam is then passed into the pan through a leaden pipe. The steam serves to dilute the acid, so that on cooling only the hard yellow crystal of sulphate of silver and not the white mushy crystals of bisulphate will form. The condition of the liquor is tested periodically by removing a drop with a glass rod on to a spotting plate. If bisulphate forms the liquid will solidify on cooling like a drop of candle grease. When the proper state of dilution is reached there will be a few yellow crystals surrounded by the liquid acid. The specific gravity is 1.66 or about 60 per cent. sulphuric acid. The time taken for steaming is 10 hours, when fresh acid is used for adding to the alloy, but three hours when the mother liquors from the crystals are used. The pan is then allowed to stand for 24 hours, or less if it is cooled by a water jacket. The mother liquor is then run off, and the crystals of silver sulphate are shovelled out into the leaden box. The crystals are washed with hot water, which dissolve the iron and copper sulphates, by decantation and stirring, then in a box on wheels, lead lined with a false bottom covered with strips of unbleached calico. Hot water is run on and about four washings given. The crystals are then removed to the drying pan; they become dry in about two hours. The dry sulphate of silver is mixed with about 4 per cent. to 5 per cent. of its weight of ground coke or charcoal and heated. In about four hours it is reduced to metallic silver.

$$Ag_2 SO_4 + C = Ag_2 + SO_2 + CO_2.$$

It is advisable to put about 5lbs. weight of fireclay or other powdered siliceous material with the silver in order to prevent the retort from being eaten through at the line of the molten charge. A retort will hold about half the weight of sulphate of silver as compared with the molten metal. The silver obtained varies in fineness from 985 to 998.3. It is usually re-melted in a new cupel and brought up to 998. The washings from the sulphate of silver are run through a box containing precipitated copper, which precipitates the silver they contain. The copper entering into solution is precipitated in a box containing iron. The silver precipitate, mixed with a little copper, is put in a box, about 20 per cent. by weight of sulphate of silver crystals is added. This serves to remove the copper still present.

$$Ag_2 SO_4 + Cu = Cu SO_4 + 2Ag.$$

This is well washed with hot water, and the wash waters passed through the usual copper precipitating box. The sponge of silver is pressed, dried and smelted.

The gold after being washed is subjected to a second boiling with sulphuric acid, in the proportion of one of gold to eight of acid. It is boiled for about three hours. While still hot the gold is ladled out into a lead lined box, and washed with hot water until free from silver. After washing it is melted in crucibles, borax being added as a flux. The cost of a plant turning out 200lbs. of dore bullion every twenty

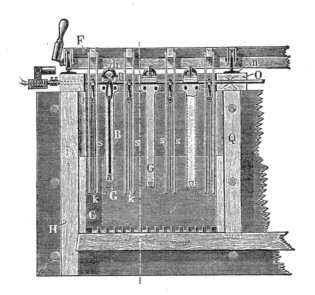

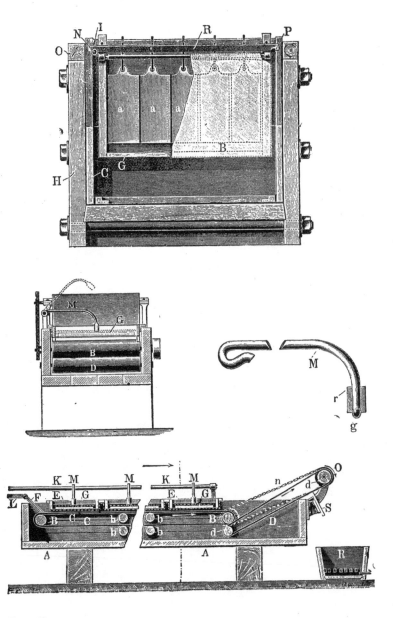

four hours is stated to be £550, and the cost of parting from 0.19d. to 0.21d. per ounce.

At the Broken Hill Proprietary works, at Port Pirie, practically the same method is adopted, the only difference being in a few details, such as in the latter there are three kettles in a row, the end ones being for the solution of the bars and the centre one for boiling the gold left a second time. Also the gold is not fished out with a ladle until the solution carrying the silver is siphoned off into the cool iron tanks. The tank is cooled by being surrounded by a water jacket, through which cold water runs. The silver sulphate crystals are washed with cold water, the washings are run over copper plates where the silver is precipitated, the copper in solution is precipitated on iron. The mother liquor, from which the silver sulphate crystals have separated, is concentrated by being run into a lead lined vat, where it is heated by means of a steam coil. The gold, after the second boiling in sulphuric acid (See "Australian Mining and Metallurgy," Donald Clark) is washed with water. It is then boiled in hydrochloric acid, to remove the iron and lead salts, and smelted. It runs about 9912 fine. There are minor modifications of this process in use at various refining works. In some the gold left after the first treatment with acids is dissolved in aqua regia, and precipitated by ferrous sulphate, in others the gold is fused with a small quantity of bisulphate of sodium and sulphuric acid; strong acid is then added to dissolve out any sulphate of silver, and the resulting bullion is washed, fluxed with nitre, and smelted. The bisulphate has the effect of dissolving the platinum present. This is recovered by smelting the slags, consisting mainly of sulphate of soda, with litharge and charcoal, a platiniferous lead is produced which is cupelled. The alloy obtained is treated with aqua regia, and the platinum precipitated from the solution with ammonium chloride as chloroplatinate of ammonium. This is ignited and spongy platinum remains. By fusing the gold precipitate left on parting with nitre for some hours the platinum enters the slag as platinate of potash.*

---

*Schnabel, p. 864. Handbook of Metallurgy, vol. I.

E

CHAPTER XI.

Parting Gold by Electrolysis.

This attractive method of separating gold from silver has made some headway, and will in many cases replace other methods of parting. One of the first processes was patented by B. Moebius in 1884.

The electrolyte used is a solution of silver nitrate, or it may be started with dilute nitric acid. The cathode consisting of thin silver plate and the anode of the silver-gold alloy usually in plates about $\frac{3}{8}$ inch in thickness. The electrolyte vats consist of rectangular wooden vessels, about 26 inches wide and 20 deep in internal cross section and 12 feet long. Each vat is divided transversely into seven compartments, and each compartment holds four cathode plates suspended vertically and transversely, each reaches to within $1\frac{1}{2}$ inches from the sides of the vat, and 6 inches from the bottom. These are soldered on to a copper rod on their upper horizontal edge, the ends of the bar projects for about half an inch beyond the plates, and are attached to a supporting hook (v), which serves to suspend the cathode from the positive (P) and negative (N) conductors of the bath, the positive pole being insulated. The cathode plates (a) are about $4\frac{1}{2}$ inches wide and $8\frac{1}{2}$ inches deep, and are cast so as to be rectangular on three sides, but the upper side has a slightly projecting lug in the centre with an eye in it, so as to enable it to be suspended almost wholly in the bath. Five of these anode plates are so arranged to hang vertically with their edges slightly overlapping so as to form what is equivalent to a continuous plate parallel to the cathode. Each of these is suspended by a double hook (h) from a rectangular metal frame (R), which rests directly

on the positive conductor (P), and is insulated from the
negative (N) by an insulating sheath (I).

Since valuable material is locked up while refining operations are proceeding, it is advisable to shorten the time
required for the solution and deposition of the silver to a
minimum. In other words the current density must be as
high as is consistent with not heating the solution, keeping
impurities in solution, or leaving them at the anode. If
silver alone is to be separated, the density may be 0.2 ampere
per square inch. When copper is also present or accumu-
lates in the solution, the current density should not exceed
0.13 amperes per square inch. The E.M.F. necessary will be
1.5 volts per cell. For the compartment of the size indicated
a current of 150 amperes, with a cathode area of 8 square
feet will serve for the deposition of 31¾lbs. of silver in 24
hours, or each anode plate of the dimensions given will have
its silver contents removed in 36 hours.

Silver is not precipitated from its nitrate solutions
under the conditions named, in a coherent form, but as fine
bright crystals, which do not adhere. These would soon
bridge the space between anode and cathode the short circuit
the metals. In order to prevent this scrapers passing between
anode and cathode remove any growths, and allow the crystals
of silver to fall to the bottom of the bath. The scrapers are
simply vertical wooden laths nailed on to a horizontal frame.
Two pairs are provided for each cathode plate, each pair
forking the plate, and so placed that as the frame (F) moves
backward and forward with a reciprocating motion the laths
sweep any growths of crystals off from end to end.

The gold separating from the anode plates would fall
off and mix with the silver were this not provided for by
enclosing them in a narrow rectangular frame (G), the sides
of which are covered with filter cloth.

A tray is provided to facilitate the removal of the silver
crystals, and arrangements are provided for lifting the whole
of the framework with the scrapers, the anodes, and the
cathodes out of the vat. The silver crystals are removed,
washed, pressed and smelted, and the gold powder, if pure,
can be similarly treated. As a general rule, however, the

gold is contaminated with oxides of silver, lead per-oxide,
bismuth. oxide, and some silver. At the St. Louis Smelting
and Refining Works, where this process was in operation, the
gold so obtained is melted down with the addition of more
silver, if necessary, and the bullion parted in the ordinary way
with nitric acid. It would thus appear as if the electrolytic
process was looked upon as more suitable for refining and
removing a large quantity of silver from a small amount of
gold rather than a separative process per se. It is consider-
ably cheaper than the Gutzkow, and has the advantage of
being worked with dilute solutions in the cold, and without
any evolution of noxious fumes.

Moebius has devised an improved apparatus for his process, the main improvements being the continuous delivery of
the refined silver crystals and the facilities given for introducing and replacing the anode bars, as well as the perfect solution of the latter. It consists essentially of a shallow
rectangular vat A. The cathode C consists of a broad endless
belt of silver 1-32-inch in thickness, which travels on rollers in
the bath B, b, in the direction of the arrows. The anode (G),
consisting of gold-bearing silver, lies horizontally above the
belt in a frame (E), covered with filter cloth, this cloth being
paraffined or oiled, to protect it from the action of the acid
solutions. The vat contains strong solution of potassium, or
sodium nitrate, so acidified with nitric or sulphuric acid as
to keep all the copper in solution. The silver crystals are
deposited on the cathode belt, and are carried forward and
dropped on to the belt D, on which they are carried upwards
out of the liquid, they then pass over the pulley (d) at (O), and
drop into the trough R. A scraper (S) serves to remove those
carried beyond O. The rollers are driven by a chain belt (n) outside the vat. The necessary current is introduced through
the copper bar (K), and flows through the stout wire (M)
attached to and above K to the anode bar below. The point of
the wire is provided with a platinum cap (g), and the lower
portion, which might come in contact with the liquid, is protected by paraffin and sheathed in rubber. The brush F
connected on to the negative conductor L serves to make connection with the cathode.

The improved Moebius plant was successfully introduced by the Guggenheim Smelting Co., N.J., in 1904. It contains 48 electrolytic tanks. The tanks are constructed of 2-inch pitch pine, coated with acid proof paint, and measure 14 feet 3 inches long, 16 inches wide and 7 inches deep. The electrolyte contains 0.1 per cent. free nitric acid, 4 to 5 per cent. copper, and 1.2 per cent. silver. The consumption of acid is about 1½lb. for every 1000oz. dore parted.

In each tank are placed six frames (18 inches square and 1 inch deep), over which muslin diaphragms are stretched. The frames are divided by strips into four sections, in each of which an anode is placed. The dore contains about 980 silver to 3 to 8 gold, and the anodes cast are 15 x 3½ x ½ inch. The cathode belt runs either within half an inch of the muslin, and is 31 feet long by 15 inches wide. At first the belts were made of silver-coated rubber, but owing to the buckling of the rubber silver belt sheets, 1-32 inch thick, were introduced. The upper surface of the belt is coated with a graphite composition, as otherwise the silver will adhere firmly in places, rendering the belt brittle and useless. This preparation is applied once a fortnight. The belt moves at the rate of three feet per minute, and about 3 horse-power is required to drive the chain and gearing which move the rolls in the vessel. A 40 horse-power drives a general electric generator capable of delivering 300 amperes at 150 volts, the actual supply for 24,000oz. of silver daily being 220 amperes at 90 volts. The silver obtained is practically pure.*

---

*Mineral Industry, Vol. IV., p. 357.

CHAPTER XII.

Electrolytic Refining of Gold.

The method just described aims at leaving gold in an insoluble state at the anode.   Other impurities are usually left there, and the gold sponge, or slimes, needs further refining by methods, to be indicated later.   By using a suitable electrolyte the gold can be dissolved from the anode bars and deposited in sheet form on the cathode, while many metals can be left in solution.   The active agent in causing the solution of the gold is chlorine; this transforms the silver in the anode to chloride, and the presence of silver chloride tends to prevent the solution of the gold by forming a protective coating on the bars.   In order to hasten the operation high current densities are employed, but this tends to cause the escape of chlorine when chloride of gold is used as an electrolyte.   This is prevented or minimised by using an excess of hydrochloric acid, sodium, or ammonium chloride, and heating the solution.   The best temperature is found to be between 60deg. and 70deg. C, with gold contents of the solution 25 to 30 grammes per litre, and with HCl. 1.19 sp. gr. between 20 and 50cc per litre.   The current density is kept above 500 amperes per square metre.   Under these conditions only gold is deposited at the cathode.   Platinum remains in solution until it reaches double the amount of the gold present. The salts in the solution are necessary for a coherent deposit of gold.   Some gold is deposited with the anode mud, and this is due to the formation of aurous chloride, which at once splits up in the presence of water to auric chloride and metallic gold.†

$$3AuCl = AuCl_3 + 2Au.$$

Silver chloride also falls together with lead and bismuth. These impurities remove a certain amount of chlorine, which is obtained from the electrolyte, the amount of gold in solution therefore diminishes, and it is necessary from time to time to add gold chloride.

The electrolyte vessels used are made of some acid resisting earthenware. The anodes are only 4mm in thickness, and are eaten away in 24 hours, the cathodes are made of thin rolled gold sheets. The distance between the electrodes, with an impure electrolyte, is ⅜ inch. This process, as stated by Dr. Rose‡ is specially applicable to the refining of platiniferous gold.

---

*Mineral Industry, Titus Ulke, p. 304.
‡Metallurgy of Gold, p. 436.

CHAPTER XIII.

The Treatment of Cyanide Precipitate.

Comparatively little trouble was experienced in gold milling with regard to the preparation of a pure bullion until the advent of the cyanide process. When ores were smelted the litharge method of elimination of baser metals and the subsequent parting had been worked out in fine detail. When alluvial gold was collected and smelted the product in gold and silver rarely contained five parts of base metal per 1000, yet some of this was introduced in the reduction of a little iron or other metal associated with the gold. The gold precipitated from chlorine solutions by means of charcoal gave fine gold running up to 998 fine, while that thrown down by sulphate of iron could be rendered equally pure by first precipitating the sulphate of lead, and allowing it to settle. Amalgam from batteries, if properly worked up, could be obtained containing only a few parts of base metal per thousand.

Precipitation on Zinc. — On the introduction of the cyanide process and the zinc shaving method of precipitation, the purity of the resulting bullion was dependent on the metals and elements which passed into solution with the gold, and which were precipitated upon the zinc. It is undoubted that gold is one of the first metals to be thrown down from such a solution. If a fresh zinc box is taken, and gold-silver cyanide solutions allowed to flow through it, the gold is thrown down in the head box with a little silver, and the rest of the silver precipitated further on. Copper in the same way appears to be thrown out after the precipitation of the gold and silver has commenced; the upper

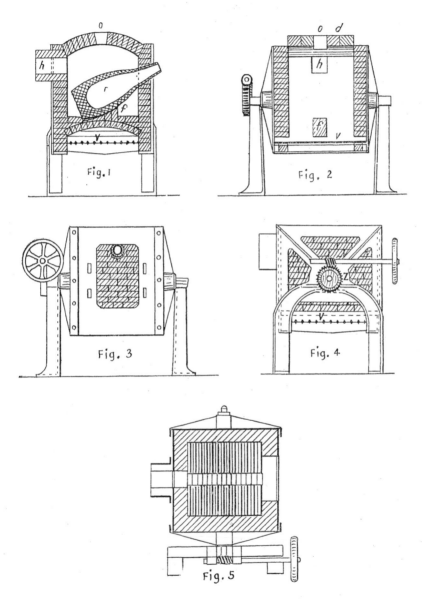

Fig. I

Fig. 2

Fig. 3

Fig. 4

Fig. 5

compartments at first contain but little, while the lower ones can be seen to be well coated. In course of time, owing to the mixing of all the material, this is lost sight of, but it would appear to be possible, were it worth while, to obtain precipitates of various grades by keeping the material from each compartment separate. Some such simple process will no doubt be discovered which will enable fine gold to be obtained as a separate precipitate from the silver.

The metals precipitated by zinc in alkaline cyanide solutions are gold, silver, copper, antimony, arsenic, mercury, lead, and occasionally nickel, cobalt, and cadmium. Selenium and tellurium are also dissolved in alkaline solution and thrown down. In addition to these elements, insoluble cyanides and ferrocyanides, sulphate of lime, carbonate of lime, silica, and organic compounds accumulate in the boxes. At first the precipitated metals adhere rather firmly to the zinc filaments, but in course of time the latter are eaten out, and the metals and admixed impurities become converted into a black mud; ferrocyanide of zinc, carbonate and other salts of lime tend to form a white crust, which on agitation makes a milky liquor.

The original method of cleaning up was to tease the zinc filaments out in a trough of clear water, passing only the fine muds through a screen. The coarser material was put back in the boxes, and the fine sediment settled in the trough. The precipitates were washed with water, dried and roasted in trays at a low red heat, the aim being to oxidise the zinc. The temperature should not rise above red heat, and the precipitates should be stirred to facilitate oxidation.* Feldtman recommended the use of nitre in drying, so as to further oxidise metals present. Very large losses, however, have been caused by this, and this is no longer recommended.† This method of open roasting with the volatilization of zinc oxide must have given rise to great losses in precious metals.

---

*J. A. Macarthur, T.I.M. and M., Vol. XIV., Dr. Rose's paper, p. 60.
†Park's Cyanide Process, 3rd edition, p. 126.

The roasted mixture was then smelted with borax, sand, bicarbonate of soda and fluorspar, in plumbago crucibles. After the charge first put in had melted, the slag was skimmed off, and a fresh charge placed on top of the bullion, and the operation repeated until the crucible is about half-full of bullion. The bullion was then poured. The fineness of bullion after this treatment varied from 600 to 900.

At the Talisman Mines, Thames R., Karangahake, N.Z., the author in 1905 saw this process still in operation. Samples of gold precipitates from the mine gave the following partial analyses. The letters A, B, C, D, E, F are compartments in one box:—

Analyses of Slimes from one zinc precipitation box, Karangahake.

	Gold.	Silver.	Copper.	Iron.	Cobalt.	Nickel and Manganese.	Zinc.	Insoluble Silic. matter.	Total Estimated.
A	1.72	23.8	2.64	nil	1.258	nil	26.00	40.0	95.418
B	3.13	32.144	4.08	2.28	2.07	1.85	41.65	4.44	91.644
C	3.764	37.51	3.68	13.86	tr.	2.86	29.88	3.20	96.754
D	0.976	28.74	8.24	6.02	nil	nil	40.93	7.20	92.106
E	0.136	16.78	12.00	10.13	nil	nil	44.78	7.83	91.656
F	0.160	19.20	4.88	nil	nil	nil	*	5.58	—

* Not estimated.

The letters A B C D E F indicate the compartments from head to tail.

These slimes were obtained from each compartment as they fell from the zinc shavings in each compartment of the box. Since the box was not filled with fresh zinc before the samples were taken the analyses do not represent absolutely the rate of precipitation, but they indicate that the silver ratio increases towards the end of the box, also that the copper precipitation takes place near the end of the box. The large amount of siliceous material in compartment A was due to defective filtration. The slimes in the case are separated from the zinc by being washed through fine gauze. They are dried by aspirating air through them, and when dry contain about 40 per cent. of bullion, the ratio of gold to silver being about 1 to 20. They are then roasted in trays and smelted in plumbago crucibles, with the addition of borax, soda, and fluorspar. The bullion runs up to 950 fine. In testing some of these slimes, after roasting, a considerable quantity of silver dissolved in dilute sulphuric acid, it is evident, therefore, that the high grade of this cyanide bullion is partly due to the oxidation of the products. It is worthy of note that while the gold and silver dissolved by the cyanide solutions from this mine is in the ratio of gold 50, silver 950, that derived from the amalgamated copper plates by amalgamation runs gold 500, silver 500.

Further reference will be made to the slimes from this particular mine in connection with other methods of treatment.

Usual Method Now Adopted. — At the Waihi mine a similar process for cleaning up was first adopted, but it has been found more economical to remove the zinc by dissolving it in dilute sulphuric acid and smelting the residual precipitate. The direct method of cleaning up has been abandoned almost everywhere, owing to losses through volatilization and dusting of the roasted precipitate, losses in smelting this powdery material, and losses in the slags, as well as the discomfort of having to smelt such a refractory material as zinc oxide.

In most places, not only are the slimes collected, but also the short zinc, and subjected to acid treatment. It is a great mistake to take this short zinc, since the cost of the zinc in the boxes is only increased by so doing. It is often stated that such short zinc is of no service in precipitating gold. This is not correct; if left until the next clean up the zinc present would be replaced by an equivalent amount of some metal or metals and slimes only would be left; as it is, such material is needlessly dissolved for the very small amount of gold still adhering to it. The boxes are cleaned up, starting from the top compartment, and the slimes and short zinc are sifted into a vat. The coarser particles of zinc, i.e., those not passing through a sieve of about 8 holes to the linear inch, are returned to the boxes.

The slimes are then allowed to settle, or at once passed through a small filter press. The solid material, or sludge, mixed with short zinc, is then transferred to a capacious vat, usually lead lined, and dilute sulphuric acid added in sufficient quantity to dissolve the zinc. The solution is kept so dilute that the sulphate of zinc will not crystallise out and prevent the action of the acid on the zinc. In Western Australia the consumption of acid is large, mainly owing to the amount of zinc unnecessarily removed from the box. The best plan is to allow the acid to be gradually added and to agitate with injection of steam. This will also serve to promote solution and to dissolve the zinc sulphate as fast as it is formed. During the period noxious gases are evolved, and should be carried away, either by means of a closed ventilating hood, which fits firmly on the edge of the vat, or else by a good draught in the open air. A certain amount of hydrocyanic acid, antimonetted hydrogen, arseniuretted hydrogen, and sometimes sulphuretted, or even hydrogen telluride and hydrogen selenide, is evolved by the action of the acid on decomposable compounds of these elements. The odors are distinct, and most disagreeable, with the exception of antimony hydride, which renders it all the more dangerous. It very often happens that the sulphuric acid used contains arsenic, and in this case arseniuretted hydrogen is sure to be evolved. The acid should be added until all the zinc has been dissolved. This can be readily tested by withdrawing some of the sludge, and after washing with a little water applying a dilute acid. If action starts then, more acid must be added. It is easy to adjust the supply so that there is very little acid in excess at the end of the operation.

The dilute sulphuric acid treatment only removes the zinc, since nearly all the metals precipitated in an alkaline solution will remain in an acid one unaltered until the zinc has dissolved, with the exception of the small proportion of those converted into hydrides and so removed as a gas; cyanide of gold and silver are not decomposed, neither is the ferro cyanide of zinc. Calcium carbonate or calcium hydroxide is converted into sulphate.

The sludge now is filtered usually by passing it through a small filter press, preferably with gun metal frames. In addition to the ordinary filter cloth, filter paper and swansdown are used to retain the fine gold. Even when these precautions are taken some of this escapes into the filtrate. This is, or should be, sent to a sump, and allowed to settle for a long time, or better agitated with a small quantity of lead acetate, and the precipitate of lead sulphate allowed to subside. It will carry down the finely divided gold. The precipitate is washed with water, and is then placed on shallow cast-iron trays, and introduced into an iron retort or muffle.

These simply consist of cylindrical pipes, open at one end, about six feet long, and 15 inches in diameter; a smaller pipe of four inches in diameter is tapped into the other end; this is led horizontally into the open air, and connected on to a vertical pipe, which above serves as a flue and condenser, and is prolonged below the horizontal pipe as a receptacle for mercury or other material which may condense and fall in the flue. The open end of the retort has lugs, and can be closed by means of a door, and bars resting on these. The precipitate is gently dried, and then heated to dull redness, and kept at that temperature for several hours. Most organic salts are destroyed, and the bullion usually assumes a light yellow colour. Very little stirring can be given to it for fear of dusting. This precipitate is then mixed with borax and sand, and smelted, usually about two parts anhydrous borax glass to one part of sand being added to 4 parts of precipitate.

The precipitate is usually smelted on large plants in Faber du Faur tilting furnaces. These are simply furnaces hung on trunnions, the crucible being placed inside, and in such a manner that it can be tilted with the furnace by means of a rack and pinion wheel, or simply by a hand lever.

The bullion so produced varies in quality according to the nature of the ore from which it was produced. As a rule, at Kalgoorlie, it is more than 90 per cent. bullion, but in other places it is largely contaminated with copper, tellurium, selenium, antimony, lead, and other metals. If the precipitates could be smelted in fireclay crucibles the bullion would be several per cent. higher grade than when smelted in plumbago pots, but since the latter are, as a rule, much larger, and are much more reliable in the fire, the sacrifice of a few degrees of fineness must be made. The slags produced are clean

if they are siliceous and glassy, and fusible, but if stony and
basic are often very rich, not only in prills of gold, but in gold
either forming part of the slag or in such a fine state of
division as not to be readily separated by crushing and panning
or washing off the lighter material.   The amount of slag
varies with the composition of the precipitate. If through defective filtration siliceous slimes are allowed to enter the
precipitating boxes, a larger amount of silica may have to be
slagged off, and the weight of the slag may be several times
the weight of the bullion recovered.   In such cases losses
through prills of gold remaining in the slags are heavy, and
there is much trouble caused in smelting owing to the great
bulk of material.

It may be safely said that unless the ore is high grade the
weight of slag is greater than the weight of bullion,   and   the   trouble   of   smelting   is   due   to   the
melting and cleansing of this slag.   The purity of the bullion
is also largely affected by the admixtures present in the slag,
some of which are reduced, and pass into the metal; others,
such as calcium sulphate, are reduced to sulphides, giving a
sulphide matte, which is often diffused through the slag, retaining a considerable quantity of gold. Whatever preliminary
process is adopted for the elimination of such metals or compounds as tend to increase the amount of slag will not only
give a purer bullion, but will lessen the cost of smelting.   The
ordinary mechanical impurities, such as finely divided ore or
silica, should be scrupulously eliminated, and the solutions
should be perfectly filtered or clarified before entering the zinc
boxes. From the clear solutions silica, which has been dissolved in the alkaline solutions, will sometimes separate out
on reaching the zinc boxes. In addition, calcium carbonate,
calcium hydroxide, and, perhaps, some organic salts of calcium separate out as a white crust, also calcium sulphate
from saturated solution; magnesium hydroxide also tends to
separate out. Ferrocyanide of zinc also forms an incrustation
on the zinc filament often in the form of small crystals. In
addition to these earthy or siliceous compounds the heavy
metals in the alkaline solution are thrown down. An impurity
in the form of lead, in order to form a couple with the zinc for

the more effective precipitation of the gold, is now commonly introduced. Sometimes the zinc shavings are dipped in lead acetate, as suggested by J. S. Macarthur; more often the acetate is allowed to drip continuously into the head of the precipitating boxes, and sometimes the lead acetate is mixed with the roasted ore as a corrective for bad roasting; the alkaline sulphides still left in the ore thereby becoming converted into acetates, and the lead remaining as sulphide with the ore. In most cases, when sulphates are present in the neutral roasted ores, the excess of lead becomes fixed as a sulphate, but when slightly alkaline solutions are used it is likely that whatever fraction of the lead is not converted into carbonate or insoluble salt, passes on with the cyanide solutions into the zinc boxes. In some mines at Kalgoorlie, where the last method is practised, very little lead solution finds its way to the zinc boxes, since the gold precipitate is almost free from lead. In other cases, where lead solutions are actually brought into contact with the zinc it would appear to be a better plan to add these only in the rear end compartments of the precipitating boxes, or else in a small tail box at the end of the main ones. Owing to the precipitation of admixed metals in the head boxes, also the heavy precipitate of gold and silver the lead, which is rapidly thrown down, can not have more than a fractional value. Its full effect would become apparent if added so as to throw down the bullion, which would otherwise pass through the boxes in solution. By cleaning up this portion of the boxes occasionally, and keeping the bullion separate, lead would not become admixed with all the bullion to any marked extent. There is invariably some lead in the zinc shavings, and this becomes concentrated as the zinc dissolves, but the amount is small as compared with the gold and silver present. It is not possible in practice to prevent the precipitation of copper, antimony, arsenic, mercury, cobalt and nickel, tellurium and selenium from solutions containing them. It may be remarked, however, that very little tellurium is thrown down in the zinc boxes at Kalgoorlie, when the ores are roasted, and simple cyanide solutions are used; when, however, the bromo-cyanide solutions are used on raw ores a large quantity of tellurium is thrown down with the gold. At the

Waihi mine (N.Z.) selenium is precipitated with the gold and silver on zinc from cyanide solutions used on raw ores.

Modification of Acid Treatment. — It was found many years ago by the author that when calcium carbonate, or calcium hydroxide separated out on the zinc precipitate, when this was treated with sulphuric acid the calcium sulphate gave a lot of trouble in smelting. The removal of these compounds by means of dilute hydrochloric was successfully accomplished. The lime compound wholly dissolved before the zinc was attacked by the hydrochloric acid. It was further found that on teasing out the zinc shavings with the precipitate that the milky liquors remained after the bulk of the black precipitate had subsided, so it was only necessary to remove these to another vessel, and add dilute hydrochloric acid until the lime had dissolved, and filter this portion of the precipitate. After washing the precipitate remaining could be added to the bulky black precipitate, and the whole treated with the cheaper sulphuric acid.

This practice was also adopted by the Homestake Mining Co., U.S.A., the only difference being that the whole precipitate was treated first with hydrochloric, then washed before the sulphuric treatment was applied.†

Use of Nitre Cake as a Substitute for Sulphuric Acid. — An obvious modification of the sulphuric acid treatment for the solution of the zinc was the use of acid sodium sulphate. This material is largely produced in the manufacture of nitric acid, and the product known as nitre cake contains a large amount of it, and may be manufactured by having excess of sulphuric acid, to contain about 50 per cent. of sulphuric acid in a state which can be readily and safely transported, and which will, in solution, dissociate into sulphuric acid, and sulphate of sodium. The trouble with this material is its liability to crystallise when the free acid has been used up. Experiments by Messrs. Thomas and Williams* have shown that the action of the acid sulphate con-

---

†The Metallurgy of the Homestake Ore, C. W. Merril, Oct., 1903.
*The Use of Sodium Bisulphate in the Clean Up.—J. C. M. M., South Africa, p. 335, 1905.

taining the same percentage of sulphuric acid is slightly more efficient than the sulphuric acid itself. It was found that by diluting the solution until it contained 9grms. of sulphuric acid per 100cc of solution that the action on the zinc was vigorous, and that the acid was soon used up. After the action had ceased the spent liquor was run off, and more solution was used, until the zinc had dissolved. The result of bulk tests was so satisfactory that the method was adopted by the Simmer and Jack Company, S.A. There is little doubt but that this method of solution of the zinc, while it offers no chemical advantages over the use of sulphuric acid itself, yet may be of much advantage where the cost of sulphuric acid, owing to transport charges, is prohibitive. Only a dilute solution of sulphuric acid is needed, and this can be obtained from the salt as readily as from the acid itself. The obvious differences due to bulk of solution, crystallising of sodium sulphate, and longer time required owing to the solutions being necessarily more dilute than those required for sulphuric acid, do not affect the principle of the operations.

After treatment of slimes with dilute sulphuric acid, zinc will have become transformed to sulphate, but lead, copper, gold, silver, arsenic and antimony are still in the metallic state, any calcium present will have been converted into sulphate, and ferrocyanides of zinc will remain, and certain cyanides remain unaltered—silica also remains.

Experiments with Caustic Soda.—Since zinc is soluble in caustic soda, according to the following equation:—

$$Zn + 2Na\,OH = Na_2\,ZnO_2 + H_2.$$

attempts were made to remove the zinc by this means. First strong solutions of caustic soda were used, and afterwards the product was heated to dryness strongly in iron pots. Not only was zinc removed, but silica and sulphides of antimony and arsenic are all rendered soluble. Lead is largely converted into peroxide; many organic salts were destroyed. In some instances it might be of advantage to use this method of cleansing the precipitate. If much silver is present it can be melted in a wrought-iron pot, and the slag, which is strongly alkaline, and easily soluble in water, used for neutralising solutions,

F

instead of caustic soda. The zinc present is usually fixed by some element, such as a soluble sulphide; a small amount of plumbate of sodium forms, but, as before stated, most of the lead remains as a brown peroxide when the product is leached with water.

Distillation Process. — The method of distilling out the zinc adopted in a few places has little to recommend it. The mistake is made of taking too much zinc from the boxes, and it is doubtful if the amount recovered pays for fuel and material. Further, unless the precipitates are free from admixed impurities, a dirty, honey-combed mass is left inside the retorts, all the metallic impurities are melted into the bullion, and there is considerable danger of loss through the zinc vapour carrying over gold. The latter danger is said to be overcome by the Sulman Picard process of mixing some coking material with the precipitate, which acts as a form of filter as soon as it has been coked for the zinc vapour.

CHAPTER XIV.

Methods of Still Further Refining Precipitates After Treatment with Dilute Sulphuric Acid.

Strong Nitric Acid. — Many attempts were made to further purify bullion slimes before smelting. The impurities present, as well as the gold, are in a state of fine division, and, therefore, adapted for solution. It might be assumed that copper and silver present could be removed by means of nitric acid. This acid was tried on many samples of base bullion, but in no case did it give the results anticipated. A large amount of the copper, and a notable percentage of silver, would be dissolved, but even when silver was present to the extent of ten times the gold, the solution was not complete. It is possible that some of the metals are precipitated as alloys, not capable of being attacked by single acids, but more likely that the insolubility of the silver is caused by the formation of such insoluble compounds as thiocyanate, AgCNS. The method was wasteful of nitric acid, much trouble is occasioned by the violent frothing which often takes place suddenly, and the uncertainty as to the solution of free gold, due to the action of nitrous acid, or the inter-action of any chlorides which happen to be present with the nitric acid. Although nitric acid may be used to a slight extent on some favourable class of slimes with advantage, yet there are too many objections to its use even as a partial refining agent.

Strong Sulphuric Acid.—The next method of purification, suggested to me by Mr. Watson, of Southern Cross, was refining by means of strong sulphuric acid. The strong acid will convert all the metals usually present in the slimes from which the zinc has been removed into sulphates.

$$2Ag + 3H_2SO_4 = 2HAgSO_4 + SO_2 + 2H_2O.$$
$$Cu + 2H_2SO_4 = CuSO_4 + SO_2 + 2H_2O.$$

It was proposed to use this method on the raw slimes and short zinc, but in this case the consumption of acid would be twice as great as if dilute acid were used. The action with dilute acid being

$$Zn + H_2SO_4 = Zn SO_4 + H_2.$$

And with strong acid

$$Zn + 2H_2SO_4 = ZnSO_4 + SO_2 + 2H_2O.$$

If the zinc is at all coarse then sulphate of zinc, insoluble in strong sulphuric, forms, and the action is not complete. Further the strong reducing action of the zinc also causes the breaking down of the hot concentrated sulphuric into sulphuretted hydrogen, and this, re-acting with the sulphur dioxide also evolved, produces sulphur. Sulphides are also produced in the precipitate, so that this method can not be looked upon as suitable when zinc shavings are present. Both antimony and arsenic dissolve in strong sulphuric acid, but the former is precipitated on dilution—arsenic acid remaining in solution.

This method will effect a cleaner separation than nitric acid, and has the advantage of being made use of in iron pots, yet the objections to it are too serious to allow of its being generally adopted. In spite of the strong oxidising action of strong sulphuric acid, there are compounds or alloys of silver which resist its action. On testing some Waihi, N.Z., slimes by this method it was found that the whole of the silver would not dissolve, even after boiling, yet the silver was present in the proportion of 3 to 1 of gold. Another objection is the large amount of acid which must be employed in order to get a satisfactory settlement of the slimes. The high density of the acid retards settlement of fine gold, and if the solution is dilute, silver sulphate when present in quantity is precipitated, and gives much trouble to remove by washing with water.

Dilute Sulphuric Acid and Air.—When copper is present

one of the simplest methods of removing it is by means of dilute sulphuric acid and air.

$$Cu + H_2SO_4 + O = CuSO_4 + H_2O.$$

Only half the amount of acid is required as compared with that in the preceding method. The air may be blown in with an injector, or even from a compressor. The sediment should be stirred by the air current from the bottom of the vat. Other metals, as lead, are also converted into sulphates, and when these are all transformed some silver may also pass into solution. The operation requires some hours for completion, but, of course, a stream of air might be passed into a vat of slimes while the latter are under lock and key.

Dissolving Out Gold with Chlorine.—Attempts were made to dissolve out the gold from admixed slimes with chlorine. For such a process to be economical the whole of the gold should pass into solution readily, and be capable of removal from the remaining slimes. It was found that the presence of silver hindered, and even prevented, the solution of the gold by forming almost impervious clots of chloride of silver, and that certain salts, such as cyanide of gold, which appears to be present, were not readily attacked. In no case was such an attempt satisfactory. In order to overcome the difficulty with regard to the organic compounds and sulphides, samples of slimes were mixed with oxidising agents, and strongly heated. In one experiment

> 10 grammes slimes
> 1 gramme Na NO$_3$.
> 3 grammes NaCl
> 1 gramme MnO$_2$

were intimately mixed and heated until a coherent cake formed. The product was then treated with sulphuric acid of such strength to evolve chlorine. After agitation the clear yellow solution containing auric chloride was filtered off. Filtration was exceedingly difficult, owing to the formation of silicic acid, due, probably, to the action of the nitre on the siliceous impurities present. After washing until the filtrate ran free from gold it was found that all the gold had not dissolved, even though a considerable excess of chlorine was present. The silver chloride formed even in the slimes protected the gold admixed with it. Experiments with other oxidising agents and acids were also tried, but the results were not satisfactory, so long as much silver was present in the original slimes.

CHAPTER XV.

The Nitre Cake Method of Purifying Slimes.

When carrying out experiments on the best methods of cleaning up or obtaining bars of bullion from gold slimes several points have to be considered. Large losses sometimes occur in ordinary practice in the drying and roasting of such finely divided material; losses occur through the feeding of such fine dust into the melting pots, and losses occur through gases and volatile products carrying with them finely divided gold when in the pots, and finally gold enters the slags. Independent of these losses is the bullion produced—as a rule it contains metals which were present in the slimes, such as arsenic, antimony, lead, zinc, copper, iron, tellurium, and selenium—sometimes one or other of these is absent, but it is rare to find perfectly clean bullion. Sulphur also forms a matte which sometimes encrusts the bar, or dissolves in the slag, carrying gold and silver with it

Experiments were directed to discover a method which would avoid the losses by dusting and volatilization, and which would either produce a high grade bullion or else give fine gold.

The fact that the gold and other metals were in an extremely fine state of division led to tests being made with solutions in order to see whether the base metals and silver could not be dissolved out in the wet way. The common solvents, such as nitric acid and sulphuric acid, proved ineffective on so many samples that it was evident that oxidation did not proceed at a high enough temperature: to remedy this, the slimes were moistened with sulphuric acid and then evaporated to dryness, and heated strongly: this served to effect the oxidation of nearly all the metals, and rendered part of the

silver soluble. The gold, however, was left in such a fine
state of division as to make it a difficult matter to handle it
without loss, and even when more strong sulphuric acid was
added and heated it was not found possible to remove the whole
of the silver.

The slimes were next moistened with potassium bisulphate and dried, more bi-sulphate was added, and the mixture was strongly heated; after cooling, the mass was washed.
The result was eminently successful. The bi-sulphate effected
oxidation and decomposition of organic matter, cyanogen
compounds, and transformed the whole of the silver present
into sulphate.

On washing the mass with water the gold could
be seen as spongy lumps, which could be washed
readily. The gathering together of the gold is an
interesting process, and is not due simply to the melting of
the enclosing salts, for when other salts which melt at a red
heat are used there is no tendency for the gold particles to
adhere to each other until the temperature reaches a point
near the melting point of gold. In the case of the bisulphates of
the alkalies, when the slimes in contact with them reach a dull
red heat large bubbles or blisters form, and the films forming
the skin of the bubble appear to be pure gold. These films
contract into wrinkled masses when the bubble breaks, and
cohere together in sponge-like form. It would almost appear
as if the gold at a certain stage passed into solution, and
formed a fusible salt, which decomposed almost at the instant
of its formation. Tests were made to determine whether gold
was in solution at any time, but either no gold, or only traces
were found.

When slimes are rich in gold, or contain 50 per
cent. or more of that metal, the bubbles described do
not appear, but the whole of the gold will, after fusion and
washing, hang together in one coherent cake. If a large
amount of inert material, such as calcium sulphate or silica
is present, then a portion of the gold does not form coherent
masses, but remains apparently attached to these individual
grains of inert materials, giving a pink powder. The same
coloured coating will be left in a porcelain dish if chloride of

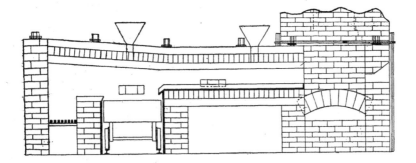

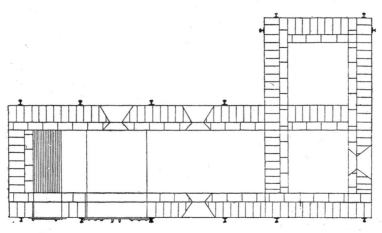

Page 94.

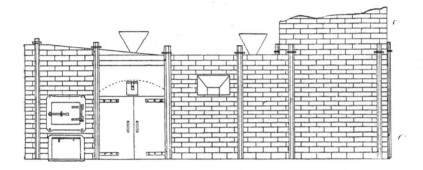

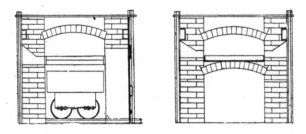

Page 94.

gold is heated with either bisulphate of sodium or sulphuric acid. It adheres so strongly that it can not be removed mechanically.

The gold left behind after the silver and soluble sulphates have been washed out, is, after smelting, almost pure.

Laboratory tests were universally so promising that operations were conducted on a larger scale. The cheaper compound bisulphate of sodium was first used, and finally nitre cake, or a bye-product from the manufacture of nitric acid. In manufacturing nitric acid excess of sulphuric acid is added to sodium nitrate in order that the temperature at which nitric acid is driven out may be so low that the acid is not split up into oxygen and nitric peroxide, also so that the resulting product left in the retort will melt at such a low temperature as to be readily run out.

If sulphuric acid is added according to the equation
$$H_2SO_4 + 2NaNO_3 = Na_2SO_4 + HNO_3$$
a large amount of nitric acid would be decomposed, and the resulting salt would only melt at a temperature over 800 degrees C. If the quantities added are in accordance with the equation
$$H_2SO_4 + NaNO_3 = HNaSO_4 + HNO_3$$
the evolution of nitric acid takes place at a low temperature, and the bisulphate of sodium remaining in the retort is so liquid that it can readily be run out. The average sample used contained 36 per cent. by weight of acid, reckoned as sulphuric acid. Nitre cake is a product which is usually intermediate between these two, or an admixture of the normal sulphate and bisulphate. When bisulphate of sodium is heated it loses water, and is converted into pyro-sulphate.
$$2HNaSO_4 = Na_2S_2O_7 + H_2O$$

The pyro-sulphate is a powerful oxidising and sulphating salt. It stands a dull red heat without decomposition, and at this temperature will attack and dissolve compounds not affected by acids which are volatile before this temperature is reached. At a full red heat it splits up into sulphate of sodium, and evolves sulphur trioxide.
$$Na_2S_2O_7 = NaSO_4 + SO_3$$

The action of pyro-sulphate of sodium of silver may be represented by the following equation:

$$2Na_2S_2O_7 + 2Ag_2 = Ag_2SO_4 + Na_2SO_4 + SO_2$$

In presence of an oxidising agent the action is

$$2Na_2S_2O_7 + 2Ag_2 + O_2 = 2Ag_2SO_4 + 2Na_2SO_4.$$

Silver, therefore, requires nearly double its weight when no oxidising agent is present, or its own weight when oxygen is supplied to transform it into sulphate.

Zinc, copper and iron, if decomposed in the same manner, require from two to four times their weight of the salt. As a matter of fact, it is necessary in practice to add more than the theoretical amount, since it is desirable to keep the mass molten so as to give every particle of slimes an opportunity for coming in contact with the solvent. A clean precipitate containing, for example, 50 per cent. gold, 10 per cent. of silver, and 10 per cent. of other metals, will require at least its own weight of nitre cake; most slimes are not so rich as this, so that usually double their weight is necessary. The cost of the nitre cake being only 30s. per ton, is so low in proportion to the value of the product that an excess can be used without sensibly increasing the cost of the operation. A few preliminary trials carried out in porcelain dishes with weighed quantities of the slimes and nitre cake will supply the information needed in a few minutes.

Effect of Adding Nitre Cake Direct.—When nitre cake is added to large quantities of dried slimes the latter are not readily moistened or wetted by the product when it melts, the result is that dry patches of slime are left, and these may be blown out by the gases evolved on heating; further, if the nitre cake contains much water this is evolved, and much frothing takes place, causing the contents of the vessels to overflow. In order to avoid these two difficulties the slimes if dry were moistened with a small amount of aqueous sulphuric acid saturated with nitre cake, or really a solution of bisulphate of sodium in a dilute solution of sulphuric acid. The mixture was made into an almost dry mass. This was then placed in an iron vessel and heated to redness; there is no danger of loss by dusting, since the water is expelled quietly and the bisulphate on drying forms a cementing material which causes the slimes to bake into brown cakes; some of the base metals, as well as silver, are converted into sulphates, the organic salts, ferro and sulpho-cyanides, as well as sulphides are oxidised.

If the slimes are wet then strong sulphuric acid in which nitre cake is dissolved is used for this preliminary treatment. The amount of sulphuric acid added will, in general, be sufficient to convert the silver into sulphate.

$$Ag_2 + H_2 SO_4 = Ag_2 SO_4 + SO_2 + 2H_2 O$$
$$216 \qquad 196$$

If 90 per cent. sulphuric acid is used the weight required will be approximately equal to the silver present.

As a matter of fact the other metals present are first converted into sulphates, and after the preliminary fusion it is found that only part of the silver will dissolve in water, and the gold remains still as a fine brown powder, difficult to handle. As soon as the baking operation has ceased, and the mass is dry and at a dull red heat, the nitre cake is added in lumps—usually it contains an equivalent of from 30 to 40 per cent. of sulphuric acid; it melts and appears to dissolve the baked slimes. If kept at a low red heat very little gas is evolved, but at a full red heat the pyro-sulphate is decomposed, and sulphur trioxide is abundantly evolved. While a small amount of nitre cake suffices to sulphatize the metals remaining, enough must be added to become molten; in that way the gold will collect and run together. The temperature also may be raised to a higher point with safety since sulphate of silver does not decompose while pyrosulphate of sodium is present. If a large excess of the pyrosulphate is used, and the mass kept at a dull red heat for some time, the gold will collect and fall to the bottom of the vessel, the upper layers containing very little. The silver sulphate appears to dissolve in the molten bisulphate since it remains diffused through it at the close of the operation.

Effect of Temperature.—It is necessary for the success of the process that the temperature be a full red heat throughout. It is only at that temperature that the gold will run together well, and that perfect decomposition of the silver salts can be effected. Chlorides, bromides, and sulpho-cyanides of

silver are all decomposed and replaced by sulphate of silver.
If the temperature becomes too high pyrosulphate of sodium
is decomposed, and the less fusible sulphate of sodium remains, but so long as the fused product on being withdrawn
shows a strongly acid reaction the temperature necessary to
decompose sulphate of silver has not been reached.   The
sample can be withdrawn by means of an iron or clay rod, to
which it readily adheres.   Since the term red heat may convey
a somewhat indefinite meaning, the correct temperature may
be indicated as that which is attained in a muffle furnace when
in proper working order, about one-fourth the distance from
the front of the muffle.   At a distance half-way in the muffle
the pyrosulphate is totally decomposed, and part of the silver
sulphate also; at the back of the muffle the temperature is
sufficient to decompose the whole of the silver sulphate.
Roughly speaking, the temperature will lie between 650 degrees
and 800 degrees C.   It is less than the melting point of sulphate
of sodium.   If too low a temperature be employed, a sample
on being withdrawn cools down to a uniform brown mass, the
brown colour being due to finely divided gold.   If too high a
temperature has been used the sample withdrawn on cooling
is usually slate-coloured, due to the finely divided silver.
When the correct temperature has been reached a sample, on
cooling, will become ·bluish or greenish white, and small
brown lumps of spongy gold will stand out from the surface.

Time Required.—When working with a few grammes the
drying and fusion may be done in from 10 to 20 minutes; but
when operating on large quantities it is a more difficult matter
to heat the mixture.   The preliminary drying and heating with
a small amount of sulphuric acid and nitre cake may be done
rapidly.   The residual cake becomes heated very quickly.
When the nitre cake is added in quantity it readily melts,
and if heating is carried on too rapidly the portion exposed
to the highest temperature will decompose before it has had
time to react with the slimes; it is also difficult to get the
heat to penetrate the mass, since while decomposition is going
on the product is being cooled through the escape of water and
gases; further, when large bubbles of gas form in such a
molten mixture they appear to prevent the material adjoining

them from rising in temperature. For these and other reasons the temperature should be gradually raised, and the mixture stirred to promote a more uniform temperature, and to counteract the effect of over-heating any part. The temperature is more easily regulated when an excess of nitre cake is used, for in this case the whole mass may be kept in a molten state for some time, and the liquid material poured out.

Vessel Required.—All preliminary tests were carried on in porcelain dishes or crucibles. These were unattacked, and gave satisfactory results. On a larger scale cast-iron pots were used, which were found to answer well when slimes rich in gold and poor in silver were treated. The pots were made from a close-grained white pig iron, those made from grey pig were too much attacked. A suitable pot for a hundred ounce trial is the well-known bowl-shaped, three-legged vessel known as a gipsy pot. This can be heated over an open fire or in a wind furnace having a small fire. The main objection to the use of the open fire is that the heating is more irregular, and that the fumes of sulphur dioxide evolved are very objectionable. If the pot stands in an assay or melting furnace the vessel becomes more uniformly heated, and the fumes escape into the flue.

After drying and the preliminary fusion, the nitre cake can be added gradually in lumps, the contents of the pot being well stirred. In a short time the lumps will melt and dissolve the fused cake. It is advisable to stir and heat until no lumps of the caked product can be felt. When fusion is complete the top layer may be poured off or ladled out on to a cold iron plate. If poured into water it will explode like matte, although it is probable that if the falling stream were struck by a jet of water it would granulate, and solution would take place much more speedily. The bottom layers can be ladled out, and, if necessary, be kept separate, since they contain the bulk of the gold.

Limitation to the Use of Iron Vessels.—When molten silver sulphate comes in contact with metallic iron at a red heat the silver is reduced. If the amount of silver is small in the parcel then as the bulk of it as sulphate remains diffused through the molten cake, only a small proportion in contact

with the iron is reduced, and even that quantity tends to pass
into solution again, while pyrosulphate of sodium surrounds
it. Should the sample carry a high proportion of silver then
a protective lining must be given if an iron vessel be used.
The best material is a silicious material which binds together
well, and resists the action of the fused salts. Close-grained
fire brick, fire tiles, or these set in fireclay, or even a good fire
clay* itself answers very well. Fireclay cemented with silicate
of soda is satisfactory. Working scale tests indicated that it
was desirable to heat the material by reflected heat from above
so as to avoid troubles due to frothing and over-heating the
vessel containing the slimes, as would probably be done by
heating it below. A furnace was designed by the author, and
subsequently erected at the Associated Gold Mines, Boulder
City, W.A. It consisted essentially of a small reverberatory
furnace, having a shallow pan for the hearth nearest the fireplace, and a flat plate of cast iron, with edges turned up
further along. The pan was mounted on a truck, which could
be run in and out on rails laid at right angles to the longitudinal axis of the furnace, after the manner of the English
Cupellation furnaces. The furnace itself was provided with a
hopper for feeding nitre cake in, and also with two rabbling
doors at the side, and one at the end. The object of the
extended hearth covered by the iron plate was to provide a
place readily heated where the preliminary fusion could take
place. When this was finished the caked product could be
worked down with rabbles into the pan where the additional
nitre cake could be added, and the final fusion take place.
The furnace so described acted well, but owing to other causes
a test made on a large scale did not produce fine gold as
anticipated.

Seeing with what rapidity the action takes place on a
small scale in a muffle, where only thin layers of the mixture
are treated, it would appear to be possible to make the operations continuous by allowing the molten material to pass
through an orifice which is kept at the proper temperature, or

*Private communication, E. G. Banks, metallurgist, Waihi mine, N.Z.

even to flow down an inclined fireclay channel or pipe, heated
to the required temperature.

Effect of Various Impurities.—The richer the slimes are
in gold the easier it is to treat them. In the majority of
cyanide plants not enough care is taken to eliminate mechanical
impurities before the solutions pass into the zinc boxes. No
silica or insoluble substance should be allowed to pass into the
precipitating box. Further, some salts are precipitated from
a dilute solution which dissolve in a strong solution of potassium cyanide. If a strong solution of potassium cyanide is run
through the box before cleaning up, many extraneous salts
are dissolved and removed, and the precipitate rendered much
cleaner.

Silica.—When siliceous material in a fine state of division
is present the first effect is to dilute the fused mass, and prevent the gold from running together; the second is to cause the
adhesion of very finely divided gold to each particle of siliceous
matter, rendering it a pink colour throughout. In fact such
classes of insoluble materials appear to act in a similar manner
towards finely divided gold as certain precipitates do towards
coloured substances which form pigments or lakes. The
formation of the purple of Cassius with tin oxide probably is
due to the same cause. The finely divided silica, with its gold
attached, interferes mechanically with the subsidence of the
gold. It is, therefore, highly desirable to totally exclude it
from the zinc boxes.

Calcium Compounds.—When lime is present in an ore
either through being added to neutralise acids, or to flocculate
slimes in decantation processes, or when the ore contains
calcite and becomes roasted, some salts of calcium, as well as
calcium hydroxide, are present in solution. If a solution becomes saturated with calcium sulphate the latter is apt to be
deposited on any surface it comes in contact with. The
launders down which the solutions run will often show long
crystals of gypsum standing out at right angles to the course
of flow of the liquid. In the zinc boxes also precipitation is
apt to take place, although to a lesser degree. Should the
working solution be highly saline the gypsum is not precipitated so readily since it is dissolved much more freely in

such solutions. Calcium sulphate is not a common impurity, but it occurs in the Kalgoorlie mines, and forms, when the ores are roasted, if calcium carbonate is present; this latter salt is usually precipitated in the box itself, due to the inter-action of the lime solution, and the carbon dioxide evolved from the decomposition of the cyanide.

When calcium carbonate or calcium hydroxide is present, it is easily removed with dilute hydrochloric acid. The acid will attack and remove either of these substances before it attacks the zinc. If a large amount of this material is present it is better removed by first washing it with dilute hydrochloric acid, and then decanting the clear solution and washing the calcium chloride out of the slimes.

If the calcium compounds are not removed they become transformed to sulphate in the subsequent operation, and as the material is so slightly soluble in water the bulk of it remains. It has the same mechanical effect as silica in causing some of the gold to remain in a finely divided state, and in retarding filtration; it also has a bad effect in rendering the fused cake more difficult to dissolve in water, since a compound analogous to glauberite forms. ($Na_2 SO_4$. $Ca SO_4$).

Calcium sulphate might be dissolved out of the solution with sodium thiosulphate, or by heating it with sulphur and water, thereby forming calcium thiosulphate, which is more readily soluble. The trouble with regard to this mode of pro-cedure was that some gold also dissolved by the action of the thiosulphate. It is much simpler to eliminate the calcium compounds by a preliminary treatment. The nitre cake used should be as free as possible from this substance.

Magnesium Compounds.—The preliminary treatment with sulphuric acid removes the magnesium as sulphate, con-sequently it does not interfere, although it is frequently found encrusting the zinc filaments in the form of hydroxide.

Iron.—Iron as such is not precipitated on zinc shavings in an alkaline solution, but ferro-cyanides form, and are pre-cipitated, or crystallise in the box, and the iron present is due to them. The preliminary treatment with strong sulphuric acid transforms these into sulphates and carbon monoxide, according to the following equation :—

$$K_4Fe (CN)_6 + 8H_2SO_4 + 6H_2O = 4KHSO_4 + FeSO_4$$
$$3 (NH_4)_2 SO_4 + 6CO.$$

The ferrous sulphate becomes oxidised at a higher temperature to form ferric sulphate.

$$2Fe SO_4 + H_2 SO_4 + O = Fe_2 (SO_4)_3 + H_2O.$$

The oxygen necessary may come from the air or from the sulphuric acid itself. On further heating basic sulphate of iron forms, or if the temperature is very high ferric oxide is formed and sulphur trioxide evolved.

$$Fe_2 (SO_4)_3 = Fe_2 O_3 + 3SO_3.$$

Usually ferric sulphate is left. When iron vessels are used a considerable quantity is mixed with the fused cake. If the pyrosulphate is totally decomposed then there is a great tendency for the ferric sulphate to be precipitated as basic ferric sulphate, when hot water is added for washing. This is objectionable, since it forms a slimy mass, which retards washing, filtration, and also the solution of the cake. It is therefore better, when much iron is present, to keep it in solution by adding either a small amount of sulphuric acid or nitre cake near the close.

Nickel and Cobalt.—These metals pass into solution readily as sulphates.

Aluminium.—Small amounts of alumina are dissolved from the sediment, which enters the zinc box. This behaves in a similar manner to ferric sulphate.

Zinc.—This metal is one of the chief impurities in the original slime. The most economical way of removing it is by means of dilute acid. As before stated, the strong acid oxidises, as well as dissolves, the metal.

$$Zn + 2H_2SO_4 = ZnSO_4 + SO_2 + 2H_2O.$$

Further, zinc at a high temperature, will oxidise at the expense of sulphates present, reducing the latter to sulphides. It is not desirable to have the metal present, especially if it is at all coarse. If the slimes are finely divided, the zinc and zinc salts present are transformed to sulphates. It is not objectionable in this state, since it will stand a high temperature without decomposition, and in this way protects silver sulphate from splitting up.

6

Arsenic.—Arsenic often passes into solution when ores containing this element are dealt with. It is precipitated from alkaline solutions on the zinc. The element itself, when treated with dilute sulphuric acid, is not affected, but in solution, in the presence of zinc, or alloyed with zinc, arseniuretted hydrogen is evolved. This is one of the most poisonous gases to be guarded against when cleaning up the zinc gold slimes.

When treated with strong sulphuric acid it is oxidised, and passes into solution. If the solution is neutral, or nearly so, it will form insoluble basic salts, with ferric or aluminium sulphate. Arsenic may be expelled as a volatile chloride by adding sufficient salt, when the mixture is heated with strong sulphuric acid.

Antimony.—Antimony behaves similarly to arsenic with dilute sulphuric acid. With strong sulphuric acid it passes into solution, but is almost wholly precipitated when water is added to the solution. It can be kept in solution by means of tartaric acid, but it would probably be easier to remove it by a preliminary fusion with sulphur and carbonate of sodium when the whole of the antimony, as well as the arsenic, would be rendered soluble.

Copper.—When copper is exceedingly finely divided no modification of the method is necessary. It may be sometimes desirable to dissolve out copper if present in excessive quantity by means of sulphuric acid and air, when only half the amount of sulphuric acid will be required. For example:—

$$Cu + 2H_2SO_4 = Cu\ SO_4 + 2H_2O + SO_2.$$
$$Cu + H_2\ SO_4 + O = Cu\ SO_4 + H_2O.$$

Bismuth and part of the arsenic are removed by this method of treatment. If a certain amount of sulphate of copper is formed in the nitre cake process, the solution of the silver is facilitated, for sulphate of silver is more readily soluble in solutions of copper sulphate than in water. Like other sulphates before described it decomposes before silver sulphate, so that the presence of copper sulphate in the final melt is a guarantee that the silver sulphate has not decomposed.

Lead.—Lead is objectionable in that it forms a sulphate insoluble in water. When fused in pyrosulphate it appears to pass into solution. It does not prevent the segregation of the gold. When, after washing salts out of the fused mass, the residual gold is smelted, lead itself tends to become reduced, and pass into the amalgam or smelted gold. Sulphate of lead, as well as sulphate of lime, can be removed by first treating the residues containing these salts with carbonate of sodium and stirring well until the solution becomes alkaline.

$$Na_2CO_3 + PbSO_4 = Na_2SO_4 + PbCO_3.$$

The sulphate of sodium, as well as any carbonate added in excess, is then removed by decanting the clear solution; after decantation the soluble sulphate should be washed out by filtration. When the washings come away neutral the action may be considered complete. If dilute nitric acid is now added, until the liquid remains acid, the carbonates will have been converted into nitrates.

$$PbCO_3 + 2HNO_3 = Pb(NO_3)_2 + H_2O + CO_2.$$

The lead nitrate can be washed out, and the solution, after neutralising any excess of nitric acid with sodium carbonate, can be used instead of lead acetate, either as a corrective to soluble sulphide in an ore, or to aid in precipitating gold in the zinc boxes. The greater part of the calcium is also removed by this operation, and the gold, previously present as a pink powder, becomes darker, and is very finely divided.

Mercury.—When slimes containing mercury are treated by this method mercuric sulphate forms, but is split up into mercury and sulphur trioxide, both of which escape.

Bismuth and Tin. — No slimes from the zinc boxes were found to contain these elements. The former occurs in the slimes produced from the electrolysis of copper. It becomes sulphate like other metals, but tends to separate out as a basic salt when being washed with water. It may be retained in solution by increasing the amount of acid present, or it may be allowed to settle with the gold, and recovered from the same by the addition of more acid.

Selenium. — Only one sample of zinc box slimes containing an appreciable quantity of selenium was dealt with. It came from the Waihi Mine, N.Z. When the slimes are smelted direct with fluxes, about one or two per cent. of selenium passes into the bullion. This has proved very difficult

to remove. It was found in the preliminary drying and heating with sulphuric acid and nitre cake that the selenium
escaped as a brown vapour, rapidly condensing to a red
amorphous powder, and that it was wholly expelled by
heating the slimes with excess of nitre cake.

Tellurium. — This element, although so abundant in
the auriferous ore at Kalgoorlie, does not appear to enter
into the composition of the ordinary cyanide gold slimes. It
is scarcely credible that the tellurium is oxidised and wholly
volatilised by roasting.   Slimes from the bromo-cyanide
process contain a considerable amount. On being heated with
strong sulphuric acid, followed by treatment with nitre cake,
tellurium is oxidised to tellurous acid.   This tends to
separate out when washed with water, but is readily soluble
in acids.   It can therefore be removed after the same manner
as bismuth, or by applying an alkaline wash.

Silver.—This metal has already been dealt with.   There
is no trouble about converting the whole of the metal present,
no matter whether present in large or small quantity, into
sulphate; but there is much trouble in dissolving large amounts
of silver sulphate in water. One simple way of so doing is
to place the fused mass on a filter spread over a wooden grid
and suspended just below the surface of the liquor in a
wooden vat. If the solution in the vat is kept boiling by
means of steam the silver sulphate will pass into solution.
On allowing any fine gold to subside, the solution may be
decanted off and the silver precipitated on copper or iron, in
the usual manner.

In order to find out the solubility of silver sulphate
when produced in treatment of slimes, several tests were
made.   The weight of slimes taken was 1508 grains; these
were taken direct from the zinc boxes. They contained gold
and silver in the proportion of 4 of silver to 1 of gold. This
parcel was moistened with 50 c.c. of chamber sulphuric acid,
60 per cent. strength, and 50 c.c. of water, and 200 grains
of nitre cake. The mixture was heated to dull redness. While
still hot 2000 grains of nitre cake were added, and the mass
heated until the whole was in fusion. The weight of the
fused cake was 3100 grains; this was broken into coarse

pieces and placed in cold water, and steam was blown in until the whole volume was 500 c.c. This was allowed to stand for a short time, and the clear liquor decanted, and the operation was repeated several times.

10 c.c. of the first decanted liquor gave 2.160 grains silver.
10 c.c. of the second decanted liquor gave 1.750 grains silver.
10 c.c. of the third decanted liquor gave 1.050 grains silver.
10 c.c of the fourth decanted liquor gave 0.772 grains silver.

The silver was wholly in solution after the last addition of water. The weight of silver recovered was 286 grains. The weight of gold recovered was 73.1 grains, assaying 994. The insoluble residue from this example weighed 320.6 grains. Another test was made on slimes containing 11.53 per cent. gold and 3.45 per cent. silver. The charge taken was—

Slimes	1000 grains.
Sulphuric acid	200 grains.
Nitre cake.	100 grains.
Water to moisten.	

The product was gradually heated to dull redness, when 2000 grains of nitre cake were added, and the mass heated to full redness. After cooling the fused mass was inverted into a large porcelain dish containing 100 c.c. of water. After some hours the fused cake dropped out of the vessel in which the fusion was made into the lower one; large crystals of sodium sulphate had formed. After decanting the clear liquid 140 c.c. of water were added, and after stirring and allowing to settle, this was again decanted; the operation was repeated for the third time with 100 c.c. of water. Samples containing 10 c.c. were withdrawn from each solution, decanted and tested, the results being as follow:—

Metals in 10 c.c. in Grammes.

No.	Sp.gr.	Silver.	Copper.	Iron.	Temperature. Deg. F.
1	1.422	0.153	0.112	0.090	67
2	1.239	0.078	trace	trace	65
3	1.073	0.042	none	none	130

After the third addition the whole of the silver was in solution. In actual practice the amount of silver in solution varies with the amount of acid present, the sulphates and the temperature; as a rule a hot solution contains a minimum of 1.35 per cent., or 13.5oz. per cubic foot. All hot saturated solutions will deposit about half of their silver as hard yellow crystals, of normal sulphate of silver on cooling.

Effect of adding strong sulphuric acid to dissolve silver sulphate: When sulphuric acid is added to the fused cake, and the whole heated, it will melt at a low temperature; but the salt is too dense to allow of a perfect settlement of gold in most cases. The sulphuric acid reforms the sodium bisulphate, and if this is washed out without any attempt to recover it the acid would be lost. In most cases, even when silver has been removed from it, it is too impure to be used when diluted for dissolving zinc from the slimes, since the metals dissolved, such as copper, would at once be precipitated.

If sulphuric is added after the sodium sulphate and most of the base metals have been washed out, the silver remaining dissolves readily enough, but the material remaining usually contains so much impurity in the form of silica and insoluble sulphates that the supernatant liquid becomes quite milky, and cannot readily be decanted from the gold. If the slimes were free from admixed foreign substances there would be as little difficulty as there is in parting by the well-known sulphuric acid process. The use of ammonia as a solvent for silver sulphate, or silver chloride which may have formed is preferable to sulphuric acid, but all acid and soluble salts must be removed before it is applied, since it will yield voluminous and very often slimy precipitates. Since both the ammonia and the silver may be readily recovered from such solutions, it can be used where ammonia is available. It is also advisable to use a small amount of it in ordinary cases, even when the soluble sulphates of silver have been washed out in order to readily remove any chloride or salt or silver which dissolves with difficulty in water, but which dissolves readily in ammonia.

Washing Out the Soluble Salts.—Since wood, after being used for some time seems to have no action in reducing silver sulphate from its solutions, vessels constructed of it may be used for the solution of the cake. The capacity of the vessel should be in proportion to the amount of silver to be kept in solution. Two systems of solution can be adopted—the former consists in dissolving the whole of the soluble salts in one operation, using just so much water as will make a solution nearly saturated with silver sulphate. By adopting this process, solution is retarded more and more towards the finish, the salts dissolve readily at first, but as solution proceeds they dissolve more and more slowly. The other system is to wash the cake in a series of vessels, each containing a portion of the fused cake. The water would be run over the first, and overflow into the second, and so on until it reached the final one. By washing in this way, solution takes place more readily, and the effluent liquor remains saturated with silver sulphate until nearly the close of the operation. As previously described, washing according to the first method is better done in a vat, a grid framework with boarded sides, the latter being dovetailed, and the grids fastened with wooden pegs, thin covered with a coarse filter. The framework is hung so as to dip into a vat of water. The fused cake is put in, and steam is blown into the solution through a glass pipe fastened on to a steam pipe by means of a rubber or other flexible joint. The temperature will rise to the boiling point of the solution, which is above that of water. Boiling is thus effected without danger of bumping. The cake dissolves, and the soluble salts and fine material pass through the filter. The solution should be complete, for if small lumps remain they are certain to contain silver sulphate. When solution is complete the steam can be turned off, the fine sediment will rapidly subside, and the clear liquid containing the silver sulphate can be run off into another vessel; if it passes through a filter before reaching the second vat there will be no danger of loss of fine gold. The silver can be recovered by various means from this solution.

When time allows it the solution may be effected in the same manner with cold water. The sodium sulphate dissolves very readily, also the ferric and aluminium sulphates, which are apt to become decomposed by hot water. By leaving the tray in water over night the salts will pass into solution, and diffuse through the filter cloth into the vat. If the cake were placed on the bottom of the vat the liquid around it would remain saturated and solution would go on very slowly, but by having it suspended near the surface of the liquor solution is assisted by gravity.

The other method which suggested itself was based on the principle used when precipitating gold from cyanide solutions, and also in the washing of carbonate of sodium from black ash. A long box, rectangular in section, was divided into compartments which allowed the solution to flow upwards through the cake placed on a filter frame, and downwards between them. Filter cloths used both above and below the cake consisted of cloth woven one way, and hair the other; flannel or felt may be used also—or even calico. Solids were thus retained between the upper and lower cloths in each compartment, while the soluble salts were removed with a current of water. In this way washing can be made continuous and automatic; the solutions escaping would also have the maximum quantity of silver dissolved if the flow were properly regulated. The washing box could also be kept locked. The escaping solutions containing the silver could be precipitated on copper in similar boxes, or if copper and other base metals were absent from the solution the precipitation could be done on iron. If copper is present in solution the silver can be thrown down on copper, and the copper afterwards precipitated on scrap iron; the copper precipitate being available for the precipitation of the silver. The main trouble about the continuous washing of the fused cake lies in the fact that a portion of the gold is in a fine state of division, and the presence of a comparatively large amount of fine insoluble compounds, such as silica, sulphates of calcium and lead. The method described for the removal of calcium and lead sulphates might be made use of in the box, but the solutions from the sodium carbonate, and from the nitric acid, should be run into separate sumps, and not be allowed to pass in with the silver solution.

Treatment of the Insoluble Residue.—When the material left after washing out the soluble salts is dried and smelted direct a very small amount of flux is necessary; for instance, in some cases silica is the only insoluble material, when about one and a half times its weight of carbonate of sodium will be all that is required to flux it. This may be carried out in an ordinary plumbago crucible.

When lead sulphate is present the smelting cannot be made in a plumbago crucible without some of the lead becoming reduced and passing into the gold. If a fireclay pot is used and reducing agents excluded, the silica present in the auriferous residue will combine with lead oxide, and sulphur trioxide is evolved.

$$PbSO + SiO_2 = PbSiO_3 + SO_3.$$

Calcium sulphate is also decomposed to a certain extent in a similar manner, but when these insoluble sulphates are present it is better to use about their own weight of borax glass to obtain a fluid slag. The addition of a small quantity of fluorspar is of much assistance in promoting the fluidity of the slag when calcium sulphate is present.

Amalgamation of Gold.—The objection to dealing with finely divided gold in smelting pots has been already mentioned. To avoid the possibility of loss in that direction, also the necessity of making slags, the separated gold can be collected by amalgamation, and the admixture mechanically washed off. When the gold is all coarse and spongy this may be readily done, but it is a difficult matter to amalgamate the finely divided gold, especially that present as a pink powder. Amalgamation must be performed in such a way as to bring the gold into contact with the mercury, so that it will amalgamate. If mercury is poured on the mass it sinks through it, and very little amalgamates, but if the mercury is squeezed through a cloth so as to become finely divided when introduced, and if the pulp is stiff enough to subdivide globules of mercury when all are ground together the gold will amalgamate readily. The usual compounds used to keep the mercury bright and clean may be added, but it will be found that cyanide of potassium is one of the best agents for the purpose. The cyanide added will also dissolve any very fine gold which does not readily amalgamate, so that at the close of the operation only gold in amalgam, and some gold in solution as double cyanide, will remain. As soon as this stage is reached the sand and such like impurities can be eliminated by washing them off into a vat, the sediment may be allowed to settle, and the gold can be precipitated in a small zinc box, the cyanide solution being returned to the mill solutions. The gold can also be thrown down as a cyanide by the addition of acid in sufficient quantity to neutralise any free potassium cyanide present, or as metallic gold by the addition of scrap zinc, and acidifying the solution. The insoluble mud, after decanting the clear solutions containing the gold, can be washed free from gold, or simply allowed to accumulate, and then added to the agitators, or to the vats, when the small amount of gold it may contain in a soluble state enters into circulation with the rest of the solutions.

Effect of Sulphate of Lead.—When sulphate of lead remains with the gold residues it is found that lead enters the gold amalgam, and will be found in the retorted gold. If it is the only impurity present it may be got rid of by methods already described. The method of treatment by amalgamation offers several advantages, and despite the fact that one step more, retorting, is added to the process, the smelting of retorted gold is a simple matter compared with the smelting of gold and slagging off a large amount of impurities.

Proportion of Coarse to Fine Gold.—It was recognised that if only coarse gold could be formed that the whole process would be rendered much simpler. In order to find out the amount of each present some experiments were made, and the following result is typical:—

Slimes obtained from the N. Kalgurli Mine, W.A.

      Slimes,   10.0 grms.

      Sulphuric Acid, 1.5 grms.

      Water sufficient to moisten.

After the heating almost to dryness, 10grms. of nitre cake were added, and the whole heated until the pyrosulphate had decomposed. The silver sulphate was washed out with water, and the fine slimes allowed to overflow into another vessel. The amounts left were as follow:—

Coarse	Fine.
Grms.	Grms.
Gold, 1.408	0.048
Gangue, 0.542	1.532

Or about 3 per cent. of the gold was finely divided.

Attempts were made to see if the production of fine gold

could not be avoided. It invariably forms when such substances as calcium sulphate and silica, which are insoluble in fused pyrosulphate of sodium, are present. The gold adhering to such substances did not appear to have gone through a transition stage such as that which came together in spongy masses. In order to see if on adding some solvents the gold could not first be dissolved, and then be gathered together, the following tests were made:—

Slimes, 5 grammes.
Nitre, 1 gramme.
Salt, 2 grammes.
Sulphuric Acid, 4 grammes.

The first three were mixed and heated, then cooled, the sulphuric acid was then added, hydrochloric and nitric acids were evolved. The mass was then heated strongly. A bright coherent film of gold appeared on the surface of the melt. On adding water it was found that decomposition was incomplete. The sulphuric did not penetrate the whole mass. The silver chloride which formed was removed by ammonia, the gold left assayed 9701, but was not free from the pink powder.

Next a charge of the following materials was taken:—

Slimes .. ..   5 grammes.
Nitre .. ..   1 gramme.
Salt .. ..   1 gramme.

One gramme of sulphuric acid was placed in the bottom of the crucible and the mixture placed above. The mass was gently, then strongly, heated until it fritted. Chlorine was freely evolved. Three c.c. of sulphuric acid were then added. The sulphuric acid, on heating, appeared to volatilize without causing the gold to run together. Five grammes of nitre cake were added, and the whole fused. On washing no pink powder was visible, but the bottom of the porcelain crucible was found to be stained pink. The gold obtained assayed 9865, but the loss by volatilization amounted to nearly 10 per cent. Nitre was excluded, and a charge made up as follows:—

Slimes .. ..   5 grammes.
Salt .. ..   1 gramme.

The crucible was charged with 1 grm. sulphuric acid, and the slimes and salt added. On gently heating, the evolution of hydrochloric, hydrocyanic and organic volatile products took place. The mass sintered and was uniformly brown on cooling; 3 c.c. of sulphuric were then added, and the whole gently then strongly heated. On cooling the mass did not alter in color. It remained brown, with no gathering together of the gold: 5grms, of nitre cake were then added, and the whole fused. The fuse was porous and dark in colour, and although it did not contain any pink powder yet was not wholly decomposed, since chloride of silver formed when water was added. The gold obtained assayed 9243, and slightly over 10 per cent. was lost by volatilization. It is, therefore, inadvisable to use salt in the fuse, since gold may be transformed to a chloride and volatilised; it is also difficult to decompose the whole of the chlorine compounds unless a very large excess of sulphuric acid or nitre cake is used. While these methods get rid of the pink powder it is probable that it is the fine gold which first volatilises. It should, however, be noted that by using a very high temperature with nitre cake alone, so as to decompose part of the sulphate of silver formed the pink powder disappears.

Experimental Work on Various Gold Slimes.—In carrying out a small test at the Waihi Gold Mines, N.Z., on slimes which carry about 4 parts of silver to 1 of gold, the author obtained a gold button which assayed 996.7. Further tests were made by Mr. Hubert W. Hopkins, A.R.S.M., and the following details were kindly supplied by Mr. Geo. G. Banks, the metallurgist to the company:—

Experiment.	p.c. gold.	p.c. silver.	Weight of slimes. Grains.	H_2SO_4 Grains.	Nitre cake Grains.	Tempera- ture	Assay of gold.
1. Slimes first treated with dilute sulphuric, then heated in porcelain vessels with sulphuric, followed by nitre cake fusion.. ..	9.67	35.95	1000	1000	1000	Front of muffle	989.6
2. Slimes treated with dilute, then strong sulphuric; no nitre cake.	9.67	35.95	500	1000	—	Dull red over flame Two hours	944.8 (Gold finely divided)
3. Slimes treated with dilute acid; then with nitre cake..	9.12	35.95	500	—	1500	Front of muffle	986.2

Experiment.	p.c. gold	p.c. silver	Weight of slimes. Grains.	H$_2$SO$_4$ Grains.	Nitre Cake. Grains.	Tempera- ture	Assay of gold.
4. Fusion with acid and nitre cake; no preliminary treatment ..	—	—	500	250	1000	Dull red	984.0
5. As in 4..	—	—	500	500	1000	Dull red	987.5
6. Preliminary treatment with dilute acid, then cast-iron added to fuse	—	—	500	500	1000	Dull red	981.0
7. Same as 4—nitric acid added, but higher temperature	—	—	500	250	1000	Clear red	994.7
8. Same as 7, but nitric acid omitted	—	—	500	250	1000	Clear red	995.0
9. Second fusion of 8 ..	—	—	—	—	—	—	996.9
10. Same as before in a shallow iron vessel ..	—	—	500	250	1500	Clear red	Gold pale probably about 600

Since it was found that a large surface of iron had a reducing effect upon the silver sulphate on fusion, experiments were conducted on a working scale to find what result could be obtained. These experiments were made on a dried slimes after a preliminary treatment with 20 per cent. sulphuric acid. The washing of the fused product was done in a pointed wooden box.

	p.c. gold.	p.c. silver.	Weight. of slimes. oz.	Weight. nitre cake. lb.	Weight. of acid. lb.	Tempera- ture.	Assay.	Re- marks.
1. Fused with nitre cake in an unlined iron pot..	10.45	38.42	224	28	7	Dull red 2 hours Fine	coarse 9887 7100	Owing to leaden pipe used in washing, silver was precipitated.
2. Double fusion in unlined iron pot	10.39	44.5	224	42	7	Dull red 2 hours	772	The iron reduced silver sulphate.
3. Fusion in pot lined with quartzite bricks .. .. Fireclay subsequently used	11.36	42.67	224	42	7	Clear red 4 hours	9887	Gold may be obtained practically fine, it is required to be at least 996
4. Second fusion of No. 3						Clear red 2 hours	997	

Although iron pots may be used when the amount of silver is very small, and, therefore, is not brought into contact with the iron to an appreciable extent, yet when a large amount of silver is present, and the molten sulphate is brought into contact with iron, the silver is reduced. Experiments made by myself in Australia and in Mr. Abbot Hank's laboratory, San Francisco, by Mr. Robert Allen, M.A., have shown this to be the case. On lining the iron vessels with fireclay, and using a solution of water glass to moisten the clay, then drying and slowly baking, the vessels were found to stand admirably. When the clay is not cemented by the silicate of soda it is apt to disintegrate on fusion, and mix with the gold, but when treated as described a coherent glaze is obtained.

Tests made on Western Australian gold slimes gave uniformly good results in the laboratory. Samples from the Great Boulder mine were treated with one-fifth of their weight of sulphuric acid, and from one-third to three times their weight of nitre cake, gave in each case coherent cakes of gold. The larger the quantity of nitre cake the more easily was the washing performed. A test was made in an iron pot using slimes, 50oz.; sulphuric acid, 68 per cent., 200 c.c.; nitre cake, 100oz. The slimes were first mixed with sulphuric and a few ounces of nitre cake, then heated to dull redness, after which the rest of the nitre cake was added. The time occupied by the drying and fusion was 30 minutes. The resulting fused product was washed as well as could be done by decantation, as no large filtering appliances were available at the time. There was still silver present as sulphate, but the residue was taken, dried and smelted, and assayd 987.3. Laboratory tests on the same material gave gold 997 fire. At the Great Boulder Perseverance mine the following analysis was made by Mr. H. B. Wright:—

Silver	5.1
Lead	5.8
Gold	23.5
Iron	0.6
Zinc	6.0
Copper	2.3
Calcium	9.2
Mercury	0.04
Tellurium	0.54
SO_4	29.20
Chlorine	0.17
Insoluble	12.40
Oxygen and loss	5.15
	100.00

A laboratory test on these slimes yielded a comparatively large amount of pink powder, mainly due to the insoluble salts and substances present. Subsequent tests of this pink powder proved it to be composed of gold and silica, no silver remaining.

At the Ivanhoe mine the gold slimes when first subjected to the dilute acid treatment, and the resulting product, after being washed with water, smelted, prouce a base bullion assaying approximately:—

Gold	70
Silver	25
Base metals	5
	100

Experiments were made from the raw slimes from this mine, 10grms. raw slimes were treated with 2c.c. of sulphuric acid, and water sufficient to moisten. This was dried and heated; 15 grammes of nitre cake were then added, and the mixture heated for 10 minutes in the muffle. The gold ran together well. On assaying duplicate samples, their assay values were respectively:—

(a) 996.2.   (b) 996.3.

Similar slimes were taken, and first subjected to a dilute acid treatment in order to remove the zinc as sulphate. These slimes were moistened with sulphuric acid as before, and then mixed with an equal weight of nitre cake, and fused as before; the gold from the samples so treated assayed as follows:—

(a) 990.5.   (b) 992.4.

The Oroya-Brownhill Company produces bullion rich in tellurium. During treatment of the ore a solution is made up to carry 0.1 per cent. of cyanide of potassium, and cyanogen bromide is afterwards added to the extent of one pound for each ounce of gold present in the ore under treatment. The ore is agitated with the solution for 12 hours. During this time the whole of the cyanogen bromide disappears. The raw ore, on which this solution is used, contains telluride of mercury, silver, and gold. These dissolve in the solution, and are precipitated in the zinc boxes. On cleaning up the slimes are first subjected to a dilute acid treatment, to remove the zinc; they are then roasted on iron trays in a cast-iron muffle, in which part of the tellurium and the whole of the mercury are expelled, and the base metals partly oxidised. The precipitate is then smelted, using 50 borax, 20 sand, and a little soda to every 100 parts of the roasted slime. The bullion produced is very base, assaying only 730 fine. It is brought up to 900 fine, and most of the tellurium is eliminated by granulating it and treating it with nitric acid. The granules are placed in an earthenware jar standing on a sand bath; water is added to cover them, and then nitric acid is added. Heat is applied for 9 hours. The solution is then poured off, and more acid applied. After washing with water the granules are sprinkled with nitre and heated in a muffle for about two hours, and finally smelted with the addition of borax, glass, sand, and a small amount of manganese dioxide. During the washing tellurious acid separates out copiously as a heavy white powder. Some explanation of this method of refining has been already given.

On trying some experiments on raw slimes from this mine with sulphuric acid, followed by nitre cake, the gold ran together well, and although tellurious acid separated out on washing, it could be removed mechanically, or dissolved up in a small quantity of acid, after the soluble salts of silver and sodium had been removed.

Experiments made at the South Kalgurli, Associated, and other mines at the Boulder, showed that by this method of treatment it would be possible to obtain fine gold from their gold slimes.

Dry Methods of Refining Slimes.—The previous process, as described, entails a number of operations, which, although each is simple in itself, takes time, and requires more care than is often bestowed on such operations on mines. Efforts were made to achieve the same results in the dry way by means of one operation; these, though not wholly successful, give some instructive results. The first method attempted was based on the cementation process, in which the silver is transformed to, and remains as chloride, the base materials being fluxed out, and the whole melted down so as to obtain gold, chloride of silver, and a barren slag. The slimes for this test were first treated with dilute sulphuric acid to dissolve

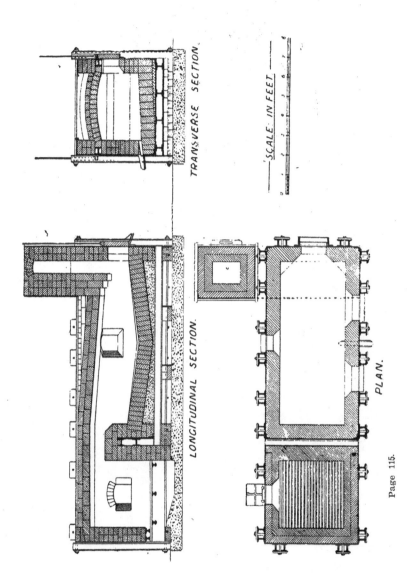

TRANSVERSE SECTION.

SCALE IN FEET

LONGITUDINAL SECTION.

PLAN.

Page 115.

the zinc, which was washed out as sulphate, the residual mass
was moistened with just enough sulphuric acid to oxidise any
organic matter, and convert the base metals into sulphates;
then a small amount of nitre cake was added to enable the
silver sulphate to stand a higher temperature without decomposition. The whole was then evaporated to dryness, and
heated until the sulphur trioxide in excess was expelled. Sufficient salt was then added to convert the silver sulphate to
chloride, and borax glass was added as a flux to remove bases
such as iron, copper, as well as non-metallic compounds. This
resulted in the production of borates, or borosilicates, and sulphate of sodium. When such a mixture was heated in clay
pots, previously glazed by filling them with a saturated solution
of borax, pouring this out, and then drying gradually, and
heating strongly, the products separated in layers of chloride
of silver, then a flesh-coloured layer of borosilicates. Covering
this would be a white crystalline layer of sulphates and chlorides of sodium. When a large quantity of silver was present
the chloride of silver formed a layer several times as large as
the gold, but the gold in this case could not be brought up to
more than 90 per cent. gold. In one case where the bullion, if
smelted direct, gave a ratio of gold to silver of 1 to 12, or less
than 8 per cent., it could be raised by this method to 87 per
cent. gold—the rest of the silver passing into the form of
chloride. Why the silver was not wholly converted is probably
due to the access of some reducing agencies from the fuel or
gases used for heating. If the slimes contained a relatively
small proportion of silver, the gold produced would be nearly
fine, but in no test was gold of greater fineness than 985 produced when operating on considerable quantities, which varied
from ten to a hundred ounces. This method was abandoned
when it was found on a small scale that gold was apt to
volatilize owing to the production of chlorine, generated from
the salt in conjunction with the oxidising salts present.

Refining with Boric Acid.—Borate of silver is not decomposed at a high temperature, and the next method adopted
was based on that fact. The preliminary treatment of the
slimes took place as before, and borax in sufficient quantities
to form borate of silver and the base metals, was added, and
H

the whole melted down. This gave a uniform slag into which the silver passed, and a layer of sulphate of sodium on top. The gold was cleaned of all base metals and most of the silver, but in no case was fine gold produced.

Caldecott's Method*.—In order to oxidise slimes more effectively during smelting, the use of manganese dioxide has been suggested. This substance has the advantage of parting with its oxygen at a fairly high temperature, while the manganous oxide produced forms a readily fusible silicate. It has also the advantage of being inexpensive. A better material is the crude manganate of potash or soda, which is an excellent oxidising agent in furnace operations, and owing to two bases being present, will form readily fusible slags. By using a sufficient quantity of this, sulphides, ferro-cyanides, and base metals may be oxidised, but the use of these materials is open to the objection that the bulk of the slag produced is increased.

Tavener's Process.—One of the best known methods of collecting, and at the same time purifying, gold and silver, is based upon the fact that molten lead readily dissolves those metals, and that any other oxidisable metals are oxidised and removed with litharge, which forms when the lead is oxidised. Although used on a large scale in metallurgical operations, and although it forms the basis of the dry assay of gold and silver, yet its application on a large scale to the treatment of auriferous slimes is due in South Africa to Tavener. The latest method of applying the process as described, appears to start with a preliminary acid treatment to remove the zinc (originally the slimes were dealt with direct). The cakes of slime, after leaving the clean up filter press, are placed in cast-iron pans, 3 feet by 2 feet by 5½ inches deep, and dried in a small reverberatory furnace; they are heated until all moisture is expelled—a white crust of zinc and calcium sulphate usually appears. The dried slimes are then sampled and assayed. As a working illustration of the process, a parcel of 22,996oz. was taken and found by assay to contain

---

*Mr. Caldecott has informed me that this method is due to his collaborator.

3150oz. of gold. The lead considered sufficient is 10 times the weight of gold present, so 29,000oz. of litharge were mixed with the slimes and 3000oz. reserved for a cover. The flux used consisted of:—

Slimes	12,975	or per 100oz.	100
Litharge	15,570		120
Coal	1,557		10
Assay slag	7,136		55
Iron	1,946		13
Silica	3,243		25

The second charge was:

Slimes	2,741	or per 100oz.	100
Litharge	2,741		100
Coal	274		10
Assay slag	1,505		55
Iron	356		13
Silica	685		25

The first and second charges were melted together, and a cover of 3000oz. litharge added.

The third charge was:

Slimes	7,280	or per 100oz.	100
Litharge	7,280		100
Coal	728		10
Assay slag	4,004		55
Iron	946		13
Silica	2,820		25

Cover, 2000oz. litharge.

The iron used consisted of tin plate scrap cut into small pieces.*

The charge was introduced into the furnace, five per cent. of the iron being added with the original flux, and the remaining eight per cent. added towards the close of the operation. After some hours the slag was rabbled off, the temperature being kept high to keep it fluid. Some of the slag contained much lead in the form of prills and had to be returned with the next charge. After about seven hours the lead was tapped out. The amount of lead bullion obtained was 28,204oz., con-

*L. A. E. Swinney, The Institute of M. and M. Bulletin, No. 26.

taining 3166.3oz. gold. The excess of gold was said to be due to that in the slags from previous charges. The furnace used was a small reverberatory, the details of which are shown in the accompanying plans and sections.

The lead bullion was afterwards treated on a cupelling furnace, constructed after the type of the old English cupel. The test is made from 200lb. of bone-ash and 14lb of caustic potash; this is moistened with 9 per cent. of water, and damped in layers into the test until it is full. The cupel is then hollowed out after the manner shown in section. A cupel will last at least over two cupellations. On firing the cupel is first gently, then strongly heated, the lead is carefully fed in at the back, and kept at a constant level. As oxidation proceeds the blast of air from the tuyere drives the litharge through a channel cut in the cupel, into a slag pot below. Towards the finish of the operation the cupel is allowed to absorb all the litharge produced. When nearly finished a flux composed of 10 borax, 5 soda carbonate, and 3 silica, is thrown on to the surface. The blast is again turned on and the molten slag run off into the pot. The gold, which is semi-solid but brittle at this temperature, is broken up with bars and melted in clay crucibles. A small amount of flux is added; this is thickened with bone-ash and skimmed off. The alloy produced from this assayed 858 to 861 fine, the balance being mainly silver.

The Tavener process supplies a means of dealing with large amounts of bullion in one operation, and when the gold is not contaminated with large quantities of base metals, such as copper, antimony, and arsenic, it should yield a bullion easily refined by cupellation. On the other hand, no operation with it is final, gold is left in the slags in the cupel, and other by-products which have to be re-treated. It does not go further than produce a gold-silver alloy. If used on raw zinc slimes or those from which the zinc has not been removed by a preliminary acid treatment, the litharge used would need to be eight times as great as the zinc oxide produced, since it takes that amount to dissolve it; the fluxes would therefore be excessive. It is also difficult to believe that no loss of gold takes place when zinc is oxidised in the air. Taking the results

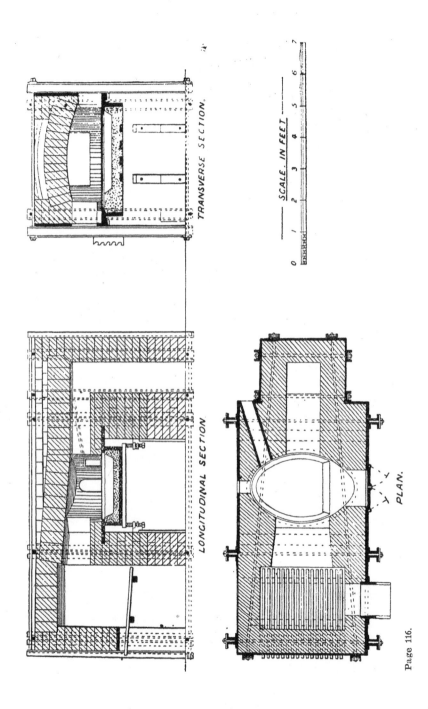

TRANSVERSE SECTION.

LONGITUDINAL SECTION.

PLAN.

SCALE IN FEET

0 1 2 3 4 5 6 7

Page 116.

as a whole they are no better than if the gold were melted in a reverberatory furnace, with suitable fluxes, in an oxidising flame, such as can be produced when using gaseous or oil fuel.

A system introduced by Merril, at the Homestake Works, U.S.A., is somewhat similar to Taverner's. The slimes are first treated with hydrochloric acid to dissolve the lime salts, then with sulphuric acid to dissolve out the zinc. The sediment remaining is then dried, mixed with litharge, crushed coke and borax, moistened with lead acetate, and briquetted under a pressure of from 2 to 3 tons per sq. inch. The briquettes are melted in an English cupellation furnace, the slags are drawn and cupellation continued in the same furnace.

Slimes from Electrolytic Refining of Copper.—Not many samples of such slimes were available, and the only one on which tests were made came from the works of the Great Cobar Copper Company, N.S.W. In the electrolytic refining of copper, plates of impure copper are hung up as anodes in a bath containing sulphate of copper and some sulphuric acid. The current strength is so arranged that the copper is dissolved from the anode or impure sheets, leaving other metals unattacked, the silver, gold, and other metals fall off the bottom of the bath as a mud, and the pure copper is deposited on thin plates which have been previously black-leaded. The silver, gold, fragments of copper, and other metals in the mud are screened to eliminate coarse pieces of copper, and the finer slimes treated for their gold and silver contents.

An analysis of this slime was kindly supplied by Mr. Blakemore, general manager to the company:—

Copper	46.842
Gold	1.450
Silver	15.725
Arsenic, antimony and nickel	traces
Selenium and tellurium	0.654 (mainly selenium).
Sulphur	2.211
Insoluble residue	9.680
Bismuth ·.	0.707
	77.369

The remaining 23 per cent. consisted of graphite, grease, and other admixed impurities.

Another analysis supplied by Mr. Radcliff, from the Moonta electrolytic slimes, is as follows:—

Gold	0.585
Silver	7.865
Copper	32.11
CuSO$_4$	11.33
PbSO$_4$	23.32
CaSO$_4$	0.535
S	3.940
Fe	0.98
M	0.205
Zn	0.140
As..	1.47
Sb$_2$S$_3$..	7.10
As$_2$O$_3$	1.99
Bi	0.075
Te	0.123
Cl	0.26
Mg	0.14
Insol	1.18
H$_2$O at 120deg...	1.74
Not determined..	5.95

The removal of the copper from the slimes is best effected by means of sulphuric acid and air. Solution takes place in accordance with the following equation:—

$$Cu + H_2 SO_4 + O = Cu SO_4 + H_2O.$$

The acid used is usually 90 per cent. strength,* but a much weaker acid will suffice. The slimes are introduced into a lead-lined vat, and the solution heated by means of a steam coil. Hot air is forced in through an injector and heating and agitation are kept up for about twelve hours. Nearly all the copper, and 66 per cent. of the arsenic, and all the bismuth and iron are dissolved. The author carried out experiments

---

*Whitehead, "Mineral Industry," vol. X., p. 229.

with 50 per cent. sulphuric acid, and found that the whole of the copper could be passed into solution if the heating and air supply were continued, and that usually the undissolved copper consisted of coarse fragments which were too coarse to dissolve within the time allowed.

The slimes were then allowed to settle, and the supernatant solution decanted. Should all the copper not have dissolved, silver sulphate obtained from a subsequent operation is added, the silver rapidly replaces the copper.

$$Cu + Ag_2 SO_4 = Cu SO_4 + 2 Ag.$$

If too much silver sulphate were added, the addition of a small amount of raw slimes will suffice to precipitate the soluble silver. The vat is filled to the original level with water, and the solution again boiled by means of the steam coil. The slimes are washed several times by decantation, and finally filtered. They are then dried and smelted with sand and sodium carbonate in a reverberatory furnace. The resulting dore bullion is then parted with sulphuric acid.

Experiments carried on with nitre cake on this class of material gave promising results. Since there is no silica, calcium sulphate, or other insoluble substances which tend to form the pink powder before referred to, the gold runs together well, even when in small quantities, and after washing out the soluble salts the insoluble compounds, such as antimony and bismuth basic salts, can be mechanically washed away. When the amount of silver is comparatively small the nitre cake process might be worked with advantage, but when the amount of gold is very small the direct fusion in a reverberatory furnace, followed by electrolytic or sulphuric acid parting, affords a simple method of dealing with this material.

The Separation of Gold from Platinum and Iridium.— The bullion containing gold, platinum, and iridium, is dissolved in aqua regia, and the filtrate evaporated to dryness in a water bath. Nitric acid is expelled by evaporating repeatedly after the addition of hydrochloric acid. The chlorides are dissolved in a minimum amount of water. To the concentrated solution, chloride of ammonium is added until a precipitate ceases to form. It is allowed to stand for 24 hours at 80deg. C. The platinum precipitate is washed with a solution made by taking a saturated solution of ammonium chloride and diluting it with one-third of its volume of water. Afterwards it is washed with hydrochloric acid. The filtrate is evaporated until the ammonium chloride crystals start to separate out. A violet crystalline salt contains any iridium present; these are filtered and washed with ammonium chloride solution. The contents of each filter is ignited. To separate any platinum from the sponge after ignition, the latter is treated with aqua regia diluted with five times its volume of water, and heated to 40deg C. By repeating the operation with dilute aqua regia until the solution ceases to be colored, the platinum is removed and the iridium left behind. The gold may be thrown down with ferrous sulphate.

Separation by Electrolysis.—The separation of these metals may be effected by electrolysis, in which a dilute solution of auric chloride is used as an electrolyte. A low current density is used to deposit the gold in an adherent form. The metals of the iridium group separate as a grey black slime. The method of separating osmiridium from gold by means of the higher density of the latter alloy has already been described. Platinum may also be separated from gold when the metals are finely divided by means of sodium bisulphate or nitre. Usually the method is made use of for treating platiniferous gold after it has been parted from silver by means of sulphuric acid. After the silver has been removed the residual gold is heated in an iron crucible with twice its weight of sodium bisulphate for from two to three hours. The molten mass is poured on to an iron plate, and after cooling is washed in porcelain vessels with hot water. The residue is dried and slowly heated with nitre to remove the last trace of platinum. The heating with nitre is continued for five or six hours; after this it is kept in a molten state for about as long. There is no doubt this prolonged heating with nitre might be shortened by the use of sodium peroxide. The gold after this treatment is free from platinum, and will assay 998 fine.

The platinum is recovered by reduction with litharge. The lead is cupelled and the platinum remaining dissolved in aqua regia, and the platinum precipitated as before described with ammonium chloride.

Purification of Bars of Base Bullion by Means of Sulphur and Soda.

Appendix.—Since the foregoing was written, the author has carried out many experiments on the elimination of base metals from gold-silver bullion by means of sulphur.   Bars of base bullions are purified most easily by adding carbonate of sodium, and afterwards allowing sulphur to flow or drip into the pot.   The sulphur may be always kept in excess by this means, the sodium polysulphide formed acting as a carrier to the base metals.   In this case, gold is passed into the sulphide matte, which floats above the molten metals, and it is somewhat remarkable that although the latter may still carry notable quantities of copper and silver, these do not serve to reduce the gold present as a sulphide in the matte.

The gold present in the matte is easily extracted by melting the slag or matte separately and adding sufficient iron. The amount necessary can be told by inspection of the reduced gold from time to time.

INDEX.

A

Air 23, 27
Alluvial Gold.. .. .. 1, 5
Alluvial Gold, Purification of 35
Alluvial Gold, Smelting 2
Aluminium 5,
Amalgam 34, 43
Ammonia.. .. .. 49, 50
Ammonium Chloride 7
Antimony 4, 6, 7, 15, 22, 60, 73, 77, 97, 116
Antimony Hydride 76
Antimonides 7
Aqua Regia 65
Arsenic 4, 6, 7, 60, 73, 84, 97, 116
Arseniuretted Hydrogen .. 76
Atomic Volume 43
Auric Chloride 70
Aurous Chloride 70

B

Base Metal 13
Bismuth 68, 97, 117, 118
Bisulphate of Silver 55
Bisulphate of Sodium 89
Boneash.. 7
Boric acid 10, 13, 113
Borax 5, 34, 35, 74, 77
Bromides 91
Bromocyanide 79

C

Cadmium 73
Calcium Carbonate 76, 78, 80, 95
Calcium Sulphate.. 76, 78, 88, 96
Caustic Soda 81
Caustic Potash.. 4
Cementation 24, 26, 33
Chloride of Sodium 9, 10
Chloride of Gold 34

Chloride of Silver 34, 40, 41, 51, 71
Chlorine 13, 31, 70, 107
Chromates 13
Clay 24, 110
Clay Pipes 28, 36
Cinnabar 4
Copper, 1, 15, 29, 45, 49, 69, 73, 79, 107, 116
Copper Chloride 91
Copper Plate Scalings 17
Copper Plate Amalgamation 3
Copper Sulphate 59
Corrosive Sublimate 6
Crucibles 36
Cupellation 31, 116, 117
Cyanide Slimes 21, 25, 72
Cyanide Solution 72
Cyanogen Bromide 111

D

Diffusion 25, 26
Distillation 82

E

Electrolysis 16, 70, 117, 120

F

Ferric Chloride 4, 39
Ferrocyanides 97
Ferrocyanide of Zinc.. 73, 76, 81
Ferrous Sulphate 65
Filterpress 76
Fluorspar.. 74
Furnaces 35

G

Gold Sulphide.. .. .. 14, 18, 20
Gold, Ratio of to Silver.. .. 1
Granulating 48
Gypsum.. 95

H

Hydrocyanic Acid.. 76
Hydrochloric acid 25, 65, 80, 117

I

Inquartation   42
Iridium.. .. .. 79, 119
Iron 1, 7, 17, 59, 65, 96
Iron Sulphide   17

L

Lead 1, 7, 59, 65, 79, 97, 114
Lead Amalgam   5
Lead Acetate   29
Litharge 25, 114

M

Magnesium 73, 96
Manganese Dioxide 36, 114
Manganates   13
Matte 14, 15
Mercury 51, 77, 87, 73, 111
Mercury, Purification of ..   3
Microcosmic Salt   11
Mints 32, 35

N

Nitrate of Soda   4
Nitre 6, 15, 24, 33, 35, 73
Nitre Cake 80, 89, 90
Nitric Acid 8, 16, 33, 42, 43, 48,
                     83, 89

O

Oxygen 11, 27
Oxide of Mercury   4
Oxide of Nitrogen 48, 89

P

Palladium 29, 59
Parting 33, 34
Phosphoric Acid .. 9, 10, 11, 13
Platinum 2, 29, 59, 70, 119
Plumbago   8
Potassium Bisulphate   39
Potassium Chlorate   13
Potassium Cyanide   33
Potassium Pyrosulphate. ..   89
Precipitation on Zinc   72

Q

Quartz   1
Quicklime .. .. :. ..   4

R

Retort   77
Retorting..   4
Retorted Gold 5, 8, 9
Rhodium   29

S

Salt 33, 37
Sand 74, 77
Selenium 29, 77, 80, 97, 117
Selenide..   76
Silica 78, 91, 95, 119
Silicic Acid   85
Silver 1, 15, 73, 53
Silver Bisulphate..   63
Silver Chloride.. .. .. 9, 53, 70
Silver Nitrate..   66
Silver Sulphate, 8, 9, 22, 55, 60,
        61, 84, 92, 93, 97
Sulphide 14, 17
Sodium 18, 46, 57
Sodium Bisulphate   8
Sodium Carbonate..   35
Sodium Peroxide 4, 120
Sodium Sulphide   21
Sulphate of Lead   106
Sulphur 14, 16, 18
Sulphur Trioxide..   91
Sulphide of Arsenic   81
Sulphide Antimony 22, 81
Sulphocyanide.. 97

T

Telluride   76
Tellurium, 29, 47, 58, 59, 77, 79, 97
                 111, 118
Thiocyanate   83
Tin.. .. .. 60, 70, 97
Toughening 6, 7, 35

V

Volatilization 34, 73, 75, 107, 113

Z

Zinc, 4, 29, 44, 45, 49, 50, 51, 53,
     57, 59, 72, 82, 83, 97
Zinc Boxes 28, 32
Zinc Oxide   75
Zinc Sulphate 76, 111

We are Publishers of Mining, Electrical,
and Technical Books.

Correspondence Invited from Writers
desirous of Publication.

www.ingramcontent.com/pod-product-compliance
Lightning Source LLC
Chambersburg PA
CBHW051242050326
40689CB00007B/1040